THE STORY OF
STIRLING

Stirling Council

This book was presented to

Ashley Jane Howard

to commemorate your

Citizenship Ceremony

25 May 2005

Provost Colin O'Brien

Grey Stirling, bulwark of the north
Parent of monarchs, nurse of kingly race,
The lofty palace, from its height, looks down
On pendant walls, that guard the lower town;
While royal title gives it noble grace.
Friendly to all, whatever be their name,
Inmate or foe, or real friend or feigned.
Danger to profit yields. How oft (of shame!)
Has noble blood her territory stained!
Hapless in this alone, to none she yields
The bliss of genial air and fertile fields.

Anon, quoted in *The History of Stirlingshire* by William Nimmo

Nimmo's *The History of Stirlingshire* was first published in 1777 by William Creech, Edinburgh, and Thomas Cadell, London. In 1817, the book was revised and updated by the Revd William Macgregor Stirling, minister of Port. This book is, in a small way, a homage to their efforts.

THE STORY OF
STIRLING

HOW A ROCK
BECAME A CITY

BRUCE DURIE

SUTTON PUBLISHING

IN ASSOCIATION WITH

Sutton Publishing Limited
Phoenix Mill · Thrupp · Stroud
Gloucestershire · GL5 2BU

First published 2003

Copyright © Bruce Durie, 2003

British Library Cataloguing in Publication Data
A catalogue record for this book is available from the
British Library.

ISBN 0-7509-3252-X

Typeset in 10.5/13.5 Photina.
Typesetting and origination by
Sutton Publishing Limited.
Printed and bound in England by
J.H. Haynes & Co. Ltd, Sparkford.

Stirling Castle. Any word from Willie?   CRAIG'S SERIES.

If Willie hasn't been in touch since 1905, when this postcard was sent, he's probably a lost cause. Let's hope he enjoyed Stirling.

CONTENTS

Introduction

A loop of the Forth is worth an Earldom in the north.

A popular local rhyme

The story of Stirling is the story of its geography. Castle, royal palace and burgh – for centuries the three were synonymous. Now it is a heritage centre and a living, working city, but for the same reasons as when it was once the fortified hub of the Scottish nation. Stirling is what it is because Stirling is where it is.

The two great river inlets into Scotland's interior – the Forth from the east and the Clyde from the west – are separated by a flat isthmus which for most of its history has been impassable marshland. Too wide to cross to the east, the Forth looped its way westward until it narrowed sufficiently to provide a convenient fording place where a bridge could be built. This was also as far as sailing vessels could travel up the Forth, making Stirling a natural port as well as a river crossing and the obvious place to start when taking goods overland to or from the River Clyde in the west. But fate and nature also conspired to place this near a large volcanic outcrop. All roads therefore led through what would become Stirling Bridge and the commanding rock thrown up by volcanoes was a natural place to erect a fort as a safe haven for Iron Age warriors, Roman commanders and later Scots kings.

As the retreating glaciers ground their way across the land they carved out the romantic grandeur of the Trossachs, whose hills and lochs were the inspiration for Scott and Stevenson, a wealth of landscape artists and a burgeoning tourism industry. What was once an easily shut gateway between the Lowlands and Highlands, calmer times have seen evolve into a welcoming turnstile to the tourist centres of the north and a triumphant monument to Scotland's heritage. Now travellers pass by on their way to tartan mills, whisky tours and a scone up the Trossachs. And, with luck, they will stop and spend a little money while enjoying the amenities.

The nearby hills have provided wealth in the form of Ochil 'Sterling' silver and copper for the small coins called 'bawbees', water for commerce and manufacture, shelter from the worst of the weather and a hiding place for rebels and outlaws. The Carse of Stirling provided clay for pottery, grain and fruits for sustenance and the country's best hay for racehorses. The rich coal seams to the south and east fuelled the Industrial Revolution. And

Opposite: A montage of Stirling showing the bridge, Holy Rude, the castle and Mercat Cross. (*Courtesy of Owain Kirby*)

These two views, from early postcards, show Stirling as seen from the Abbey Craig, site of the National Wallace Monument. The upper picture shows the characteristic crag and tail formation of a volcanic plug with debris deposited when glaciers slid over and around it. The top of the dolerite crag is the obvious site for a castle and the burgh naturally developed down the tail, later surrounding the hill on flatter land. (*BD*)

The loops and windings of the River Forth, uncrossable until it narrows in Stirling itself. It is easy to imagine these fields, now drained and cultivated, as impassable marshlands. This was a barrier to passage north and south and accounts for Stirling's early strategic importance and its later significance in trade and as a gateway to the Highlands. (*SCLS*)

if the microclimate is, to say the least, idiosyncratic, it is tolerant of agriculture and industry alike.

Stirling is, of course, in Scotland. And it is a kind of cultural capital for Scotland. It makes much of its living from the reputation of three of the four most potent Scottish cultural icons – Wallace, Bruce and Mary, Queen of Scots, the other being Robert Burns, who has a statue in the town and engraved a poem on a pub window, so even he can be claimed. Add Kenneth MacAlpin, Bonnie Prince Charlie and Rob Roy and it seems like a microcosm of all Scottish history. And the history is due in large measure to the people who lived it.

Who on Earth are the Scots?

Scotland is a rather unique place. Geologically it has more in common with Newfoundland and the Appalachians than with the rest of Britain. Culturally, it is a different planet – England has no national costume and Wales has no national drink, while Scotland has both in abundance. Politically it is a world away from Westminster. Scotland is a nation, but not a state. The Scots have governance but not government. There is a unified civil society but a diverse ethnic and linguistic admixture, stemming from

its origins in settlements of Celts, Picts, Britons, Gaels, Vikings, Anglo-Saxons and Normans.

Despite its apparent cohesiveness, Scotland remains stubbornly heterogeneous – the urban Stirling city-dweller of today has little in common with the Gaelic-speaking West Highland Free Church minister or the Kelvinside-accented Glasgow merchant, who in turn have few points of contact with the Borders farmer or the Lallans-talking East Neuk fisherman. This is one of many reasons why Scotland has proved so difficult to subjugate, legislate for, rule over, control or pacify. Wha's like us, eh?

When Stirling ceased to be a royal palace the town had to find its own way as a burgh and gradually spilled down the castle rock. As tourism and industry grew in importance, Stirling naturally became the administrative and commercial fulcrum for the Forth Valley and in the 1960s home to a university. Finally, in 2002, the historical and contemporary importance of Stirling was recognised in its new status as a city. It certainly has a better claim to this singular honour than Paisley, Ayr or Dumfries, and possibly more so than Inverness or Perth.

The great thing about Stirling, its crowning virtue, is precisely that it isn't anywhere else. Because if it were, it just wouldn't be Stirling.

Stirling is inland, yet it was a thriving port for imports and exports and later – as seen in this 1900s postcard – the pleasure-boating trade. (*SCLS*)

1

The First 600 Million Years

The Physical Geography of Stirling

In 1603 Scotland took over England, when James VI became James I. By 1707 it was practically a client state of the Westminster Parliament. Almost 400 years later in 1998, the beginnings of re-separation were evident in Scottish devolution. But Scotland and England have always been very distinct. Even the very rocks from which they are made came from different parts of the world, brought together by plate tectonics. Today Scotland and England are firmly joined in the earth's temperate zone, but in the Cambrian period 550 million years ago, when multi-cellular life started to proliferate, they were both in the southern hemisphere.

To the south was what became England, Wales and southern Ireland, while 3,000 miles north was the American continent, and the rocks of Scotland. Newfoundland marks where one of the earth's great continental plates split apart about 600 million years ago and then collided again some 200 million years later. Scotland bumped into Europe, and stuck. The join occurs, interestingly, not far from where Hadrian's Wall was later built. Mud from the vanished ocean was squeezed and raised, becoming the hills of the Borders, while the collision threw up the Caledonian Mountains. Their eroded remains are now the Scottish Highlands which start not far north of Stirling.

The melting crust of 500 and 400 million years ago formed underground vats of molten rocks which cooled and became the characteristic granites. An ice cap developed at the South Pole and four-legged vertebrates evolved in the coal swamps near the equator, where Scotland was now positioned. Scotland carried on north past the equator until, in the Carboniferous era about 340 million years ago, corals lived in the tropical coastal seas and central Scotland was dominated by volcanoes, including the ones that formed the rocks of Edinburgh Castle and Stirling Castle. Volcanic lava produces fertile soil and the tropical forests eventually became Scotland's coal and oil.

By 260 million years ago, Britain had moved north again. The high lava plateaus and the great Scottish desert saw very little life, and there was no Atlantic Ocean. Reptiles spread across the face of the Pangaea supercontinent

but the greatest extinction event ever wiped out 99 per cent of all life. Those reptiles that would later dominate as the dinosaurs started to develop in the coal swamps to fill the niche. Further land movements opened the Atlantic Ocean as the American plate drifted away, leaving behind the rock that became Scotland but pulling away its geological cousin, Newfoundland. By the time the large dinosaurs died out (or rather, evolved) 65 million years ago, volcanoes began to cool, leaving great crags of lava outcrops. Scotland was near its present position and the stage was set for the great Ice Age.

The Scottish mountains were then as high as the much younger Himalayas are now. But huge sweeps of ice gouged and scraped the land, eroding the mountains to the mere 3,000-foot stumps we see today. The landscape was still in the grip of frost 12,000 years ago, until the glaciers – moving rivers of ice – receded northwards, leaving behind a completely barren country. There were no trees, not even grass, but rainfall washing soil off the denuded hillsides into the newly formed lochs and valleys. Although the earth's average surface temperature has remained a more or less constant 20 °C for most of the 3,600 million years life has existed, an ice age happens every 150 million years or so, with glacials and interglacials (cold and warm phases) lasting 100,000 years or so per cycle. The current interglacial began in perhaps 10,000 BCE (Before Common Era, that is before the year 0) and defined what we consider the Holocene (historical) epoch.

Where once there was ice, now sheep may safely graze. Glaciers scoured the land flat, producing a fertile flood plain. This 1901 postcard shows how the land now called the King's Park was suitable initially for hunting and later for grazing. (*BD*)

From the Stone Age to the Iron Age

Liberated of 300 feet of ice, the land lifted and as the melt water started to fill what would become the North Sea, the terrain of central Scotland was exposed. On their way to the ocean the retreating glaciers had swept around and between the dolerite crags of Stirling Rock and Abbey Craig – site of the Wallace Monument – leaving flat marshes swept by the loops of the River Forth. The melting ice deposited its debris on the far side of the volcanic plug, leaving the distinctive crag and tail formations evident today.

Wind-blown seeds created vegetation and habitats where birds and other animals could live, and following the animals, human hunter-gatherer groups arrived, probably originating in Asia and passing through Europe before reaching Britain and Ireland. The climate was several degrees warmer than today so these peoples could live comfortably in caves or temporary structures while hunting the plentiful reindeer, mammoth and bison, which were eventually replaced by woodland species such as red deer and wild boar.

During the Neolithic period (4400–2000 BCE) there was very little difference between the Neolithic inhabitants and the incoming 'Beaker People'. But where did they get bronze? Scotland had several sources of both copper and gold. Copper was found in the Ochil Hills near Stirling and elsewhere but bronze requires tin and the only source of this in Britain is in Cornwall. This indicates contact between Scotland and the south-west of England (as well as Ireland, where finished artifacts have been found).

A warrior aristocracy, now known as Celtic, appeared in about 700 BCE, or at least it is assumed they came. Just because we have Japanese cars, televisions and children's games does not mean the Japanese have invaded Britain. Undoubtedly there was acculturation, with the techniques and practices of the Celts filtering into the lives of the Bronze Age inhabitants. One thing they certainly brought with them was the Iron Age and new weapons like swords and shields. As Winston Churchill put it, 'Men armed with iron entered Britain and killed the men of bronze.' This inevitably led to a need for easily defended settlements. The Celts, an enlightened, cultured people with a talent for metal-working and agriculture, introduced three typical structures – 'crannogs' (artificial islands usually found in lochs); 'duns' (oval or circular stone-walled forts); and timber forts and later hundreds of 'brochs' (large towers built of stone with internal walls divided into compartments). It is inconceivable that a natural citadel like Stirling rock would not be the site of one of these.

At Julius Caesar's first invasion of Britain in 55 BCE, Scotland was divided between a number of warring Iron Age tribes, who spent their time raiding each other, growing oats and barley, raising sheep, fishing for river salmon and hunting deer. It would be half a dozen generations or so before the Romans reached Scotland and made their presence felt near Stirling. However, news of the vast army of well-disciplined warriors must have reached the people they would later write into their history as the Picts.

The Romans are Coming!

In Scotland the Romans left very little behind compared with the network of roads, aqueducts, camps and villas that cover England. Their dominion over Britain never extended much further than Stirling, and their presence even that far was sporadic and fragile. However, they effectively caused the disparate tribes to forge themselves into more or less a nation, centred near Stirling, possibly in Fortriu (Forteviot). Pictland, if it ever existed as such, was a response to Roman aggression and led directly to the creation of the Scottish realm.

There is considerable evidence of Roman presence in Stirlingshire – a string of forts, *praesidia*, from the west coast to Camelon and Castlecary, a paved road along the same route then north through Stirling and, best known of all, the Antonine Wall. But it is not clear to what extent the Romans occupied Stirling itself. There are records of an inscription on a stone opposite the old gate of the castle, found by the eighteenth-century doctor and antiquarian Sir Robert Sibbald, but now obliterated. It read '*In Excv. Agit. Leg. II.*', which Sibbald suggests is '*In excubias agitantes legionis secunda*' – 'for the daily and nightly watch of the Second Legion'.

There is every reason why the Romans would have occupied the crag of the castle rock. If it were already a hill fort of the local Celtic tribes, it would need to be taken before the legions could proceed northwards. If unoccupied, it is unlikely the Romans would not have seen its defensive potential. Possibly the

Gnaeus Julius Agricola, during whose time the Roman invasions of Scotland began, is seen here in a much later and whimsical engraving of the eighteenth century. (*BD*)

How others see us – a fanciful depiction of a 'fierce Caledonian' from a sixteenth-century travel book, based on Roman descriptions. (*BD*)

best evidence that it was already a fortified citadel is that the Romans did not include it in their string of defences along the isthmus between the rivers they called Glota (Clyde) and Bodotria (Forth) or in the Antonine Wall. Perhaps they had had to establish themselves a little way to the south in order to mount a campaign against it. They may, however, have sited a fort nearby at Allauna (sometimes identified with Bridge of Allan but possibly further north).

The Romans produced the first written accounts of the peoples of Scotland. In 79 CE (Common Era, that is after the year 0) the eleventh Roman Governor of Britannia, Gnaeus Julius Agricola, was ordered by Emperor Titus to advance north. Tacitus, Agricola's son-in-law and the biographer and propagandist, recorded his various campaigns in the north in about 98 CE.

In the second century CE the geographer Ptolemy drew up the first known map of Scotland, which identified seventeen tribal territories, on what basis we do not know. Other descriptions show that the Romans regarded the 'barbarian' Picts with their customary mixture of fear, contempt and glimpses of awe. Dio Cassius wrote in 197 CE that: 'They live in huts, go unclothed and unshod. They have a mainly democratic government, and are addicted to robbery. They can withstand hunger and cold and all hardships; they will retreat into their marshes and stand firm for days with only their heads above

THE ANTONINE WALL

Hadrian had built his wall between the Solway and the Tyne in about 117–122 CE, effectively declaring it the northern extent of the Roman Empire. Hadrian's successor, Antoninus Pius, determined to push the frontier north to the Forth–Clyde isthmus and commanded the construction of his own wall, the Antonine. This was built by Lollius Urbicus in about 142–144 CE and ran for about 40 miles from Velunia (Carriden) on the River Forth to Credigone (Old Kilpatrick) on the Clyde. The Sixth and Twentieth legions, with additional auxiliary troops, took two years to construct the 36 miles of ditch, rampart and roadway and the twenty or so forts. The engineers who later built the Forth–Clyde Canal and the Edinburgh–Glasgow Railway used the same line.

The wall would have consisted of a turf rampart to a height of about 20 feet on a 24-foot stone base behind a deep defensive ditch on its northern side, 20 feet deep and 40 feet wide, which could have been filled with water in the case of attack. A road atop ran for 39,726 Roman paces (36 miles, 620 yards), which had about 20 forts along its length – 3 at each end and 1 every 2 miles between – and some 40 *praesidia* and other defensive structures, some possibly sited on forts used by Agricola before his invasion of Scotland in 83 CE. Beacons positioned strategically along the wall were a warning system in the event of aggression. The forts were connected by a Roman military way, running along the southern side.

The Antonine Wall was intended to protect the province of Britannia from the Caledonian tribes. To cross the wall they would have to cross the ditch, breach the defences and mount the wall itself. If they managed that, the Romans would cut them off by moving troops along the military way from the larger garrisons. The wall was also a customs post where trade had to pass through the gates of the forts and pay tolls. Settlements near the forts would undoubtedly have made a living from supplying the troops with local merchandise as well as cross-border trade. This was also a way to gather intelligence.

Soon after the Emperor Antoninus died, his successor, Marcus Aurelius, moved the frontier back south to the more easily defended Hadrian's Wall. The Antonine Wall was built mainly for the prestige of expanding the Empire and the glory of Antoninus as Emperor. It bore little reality to the strategic or political needs of the Roman occupation of Britain. The symbol of Antoninus's 'conquest' was neither necessary nor required.

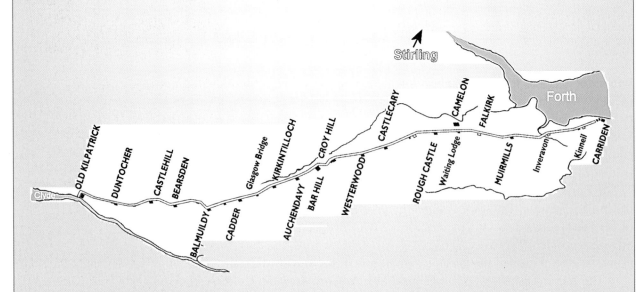

The Antonine Wall stretched across the Clyde–Forth isthmus from Old Kilpatrick on the Clyde to Carriden on the Forth.

This neat propaganda piece is taken from a distance stone, depicting a cavalryman from the Second Legion 'Augusta' dispensing with the local barbarians. The Second Legion built this section of the wall, near Bridgeness and may have occupied Stirling Castle rock.

If anything, it was an embarrassing reminder of failure. It was occupied for just twenty-five years. One of the best preserved areas of the ditch is at Watling Lodge, near Stirling.

If the intention of the Antonine Wall was to ensure peace, it worked in a sense. For most of the next two centuries the border was peaceable and the Romans traded with the tribes north of Hadrian's Wall. But it also had the effect of uniting the British Votadini and Selgovae of the Borders, the Dumnonii of Strathclyde, the Novantae of Galloway and possibly the Picts around Stirling into a confederation collectively known as the Maeatae (this name survives in Dumyat and Myot Hill, near Stirling). The Romans and the locals left each other alone from 164 to 197 CE, until the natives grew restless and started pressing the invaders at Hadrian's Wall. It was roughly at this time when Dio Cassius makes reference to the Maeatae, living just beyond the Antonine Wall, and the Caledonians further north. During the three-year period from 208 to 211 CE the local tribes waged guerrilla war against the Emperor Septimus Severus, who came in person with his sons Caracalla and Geta to deal with the insurrection. He based at Carpow on the southern bank of the Tay (near what is now Abernethy, about 35 miles north-west of Stirling) and may have reached as far north as Stonehaven. He briefly reoccupied and repaired portions of the Antonine Wall, but again could not hold it. The Caledonii and Maeatae had to come to terms, but when Severus died in 211 his sons returned to Rome and the border again reverted to Hadrian's Wall. The campaign ended and there was no further frontier conflict for a century.

water, and in the forests they will live on barks and roots.' That may be. The fact remains that the Romans made little headway into Scotland and never subdued it as they had the rest of Britain.

Agricola's legions may well have based themselves at Camelon, about 10 miles south of Stirling and near present-day Falkirk. From there his boats could bring supplies from the Forth by the River Carron. The Pictish Caledonian tribes around Stirling and further north, faced with imminent invasion by the most efficient military machine in the world, decided not to take it lying down as their cousins in the south of Britain largely had. According to Tacitus, the Caledonians 'turned to armed resistance on a large scale' – they attacked Roman forts, mounted skirmishing raids against the legions and in one nocturnal surprise attack very nearly wiped out the whole ninth legion. In any event, Agricola was retired and Lucullus named governor in his stead. All forts in the Forth and Clyde Valley were abandoned and the perimeter of the Empire was just north of the Cheviot hills. Later, this was consolidated into the Antonine Wall.

The Emergence of the Picts

Ptolemy identified as many as twelve different tribes inhabiting northern Britain at the time of the Roman invasions. It has been suggested that the presence of the Romans, in a sense, created the Picts, forcing the various northern tribes to unite into one confederation in self-defence, as happened with the Maeatae.

The names of the Pictish kingdoms come from various places and are roughly in accord with the foundation myth of seven Pictish kings descended from the 'first' Pict, known in Gaelic sources as Cruithne (also the Gaelic

The 1,373-foot Dumyat Hill, in the Ochils near Stirling, may be named from the Celtic/Pictish Maeatae. It serves as a warning beacon, a trig point for surveys, a cairn and a memorial, emphasising the continuity of use from pre-history until now. (NP)

name for the Picts in general). One of these is no less an authority than St Columba, whose stanza appears in the eleventh-century Irish *Lebor Bretnach* (*Book of Britain*) and *Lebor Gabála Érenn* (*Book of the Taking of Ireland*):

> Morsheiser do Cruithne clainn
> raindset Albain i secht raind:
> Cait, Ce, Cirig, cetach clann,
> Fib, Fidach, Fotla, Fortrenn.

This might be translated as:

> Seven of Cruithne's children
> divided Alba into seven parts:
> Cait, Ce, Cirig (Circinn, children with hundreds of possessions),
> Fib, Fidach, Fotla and Fortriu.

Some of these names survive – for example Caithness (Cait), Atholl (Fotla), Glenfiddich (Fidach) and Fife (Fib). Fortriu – the Pictish kingdom that would have included Stirling – might be cognate with Verturiones (the Roman name for an earlier tribe) and with the name of the River Forth.

The Roman Legions Depart and Scotland Invents England

Faced with an alliance of Picts, Scots and Saxons, the Romans basically gave up trying to control the land north of Hadrian's Wall. In 411 CE the legions left to deal with the barbarian crisis at home. The Romanised Britons (who by now considered themselves more Roman than British) appealed constantly for help to no avail and eventually had to hire other 'barbarians' – in this case, the Angles and Saxons – to assist them. These Germanic tribes later settled and eventually dominated the land south of Hadrian's Wall. It is surely one of history's greatest ironies that the Roman civilisation all but disappeared and that the solution to Scottish tribal raids actually brought into Britain the very people who would create 'England'.

The power vacuum left by the Romans boiled for almost three centuries, culminating in the crushing victory of King Brudei and his Picts over King Ecgfrith of Northumbria in the mid-600s. The Northumbrian army was routed, most of them killed or enslaved, 'English' influence retreated south of the Forth and a unified state was starting to emerge in northern Britain. This would be consolidated over the next two centuries, culminating in the kingdom of Scotland under Kenneth MacAlpin, in which Stirling played so great a part.

Recently, Dark Age Stirling thrust itself into history when it was discovered that there had been a timber-laced fortress on Abbey Craig dating from 500 to 780 CE. Found while workmen were laying cables for floodlights at the Wallace Monument, the citadel has all the signs of a heavily fortified tribal capital. Stirling was clearly an important centre at just about the time Scotland as a political entity was coming into existence.

2

Stirling Castle –
From Citadel to Royal Palace

A huge brooch, clasping Highlands and Lowlands together.

Alexander Smith, 1856

Stirling is the greatest of Scotland's castles. Superficially alike in shape and layout to its larger but less appealing cousin in Edinburgh, it occupies a similar position – atop a large volcanic crag – and for similar reasons. The castle dominates the skyline of the area and affords an uninterrupted view for miles around in every direction. It commands the lowest crossing point of the River Forth and the highest navigable point. The Romans knew this when they fortified Camelon so their fleet could bring provisions up the River Carron to within a short distance. Its site is also near the shortest land distance between the Forth and Clyde, but to the west and north the marshes were practically impassable. Stirling Castle is therefore at the crossroads of both the strategic way north–south and the trade routes on land and water. For this reason, Stirling played a crucial part in the early forging of Scotland as a nation. Not for nothing has it been called 'the key to Scotland'.

Scotland and Alba

Some time before 850, the Picts of central and east Scotland and the Gaelic Scots of Dalriada (roughly present-day Argyll) came together as one nation. Scottish history is often depicted as starting with the death of Alpin and the ascendancy of his son Kenneth MacAlpin who ruled Dalriada from 834 and Pictavia from about 841 to 849, but this is more a convenience rather than an historical milestone. Almost nothing is known of Alpin, save his birth possibly in 810 and his crushing defeat of the Picts in 834. Kenneth, although never actually crowned king, is generally given credit for uniting the Scots and the Picts in 844 and history has dubbed him Kenneth I. In fact, there had been many intermarriages and alliances between the various Scot and Pictish tribes

or kingdoms for centuries before and Kenneth also had a claim to the Pictish throne through matrilineal succession (his mother was a Pictish princess).

Legend tells that Kenneth besieged a stronghold at Stirling some time after 842, which suggests a fort already existed on the castle site, or perhaps at the Abbey Craig site mentioned on p. 9. One battle is said to be connected with a 'Gathering Stone' on land that once belonged to Airthrey Castle but is now owned by the University of Stirling. The Gathering Stone itself is wreathed in confusion. It is said to have been used either as a mustering point for the Picts in a battle with Alpin in 834, or his son Kenneth MacAlpin in 843 or raised as a monument to either of their victories. More likely, it is an older standing stone. There is no proven connection with the battle and no real evidence that a battle actually took place at Airthrey at all. However, this has not prevented the stone becoming the site and subject of a later struggle. In 2002 the university decided on the need for two new rugby pitches and, after consultations with Historic Scotland and Stirling Council planners, was given permission to lay these near the stone. The university has pledged to preserve and protect the stone, with a 15-metre 'exclusion zone' and a path to improve public access, but there was a vigorous protest at the time.

What is known is that Kenneth did conquer this land – he defeated the Picts near Cambuskenneth in 843 – and moved the centre of his new kingdom into the heart of Pictland, possibly at Forteviot, between Stirling and

The origin of the name Stirling may be Stryveling, meaning 'strife', from the many contests of which it was the subject and the scene. Another theory is that is refers to the 'strife' at the confluence of three rivers – the Forth, the Teith and Allan Water. Alternatively, the source may be from the Gaelic Strulia, meaning a river crossing. (BD)

The Gathering Stone. It was possibly a mustering point for the Picts during the ninth century. (*University of Stirling*)

Perth. Also harried by Vikings in the west, Kenneth shifted the focus of the new nation of Alba eastwards. He also moved the relics of St Columba from vulnerable Iona to Dunkeld and established nearby Scone as the site of coronation for all Scottish kings thereafter. He is credited with installing the Stone of Destiny there, although this is not certain. The area served by the rivers Forth, Earn and Tay – roughly Stirlingshire and Perthshire today – thus became the centre of Scotland. From there, Kenneth waged a series of wars against Saxons, Britons, Danes and Vikings and made and broke a variety of alliances in the process of forging the Scottish nation.

It is often said that the Pictish kingdom disappeared at this point. Certainly all Pictish artifacts and stoneworks and their inscriptions date from before this time. But really, the Picts didn't 'disappear' any more than the culture that played dominoes and listened to the radio by gas light in the 1920s 'disappeared' to be replaced by one with computer games, television and electric lighting – one became the other by assimilating external influences. The Scots were a literate and intellectually influential people (Charlemagne recruited Scots to fill his chairs of Philosophy, Mathematics and Languages in his new University of Paris). Therefore it is not surprising that it was the writings of the Scots that survived rather than the stone carvings and folk memory of the Picts, just as our computer records will survive better than the printed papers of our ancestors. But what did disappear was the Dalriada kingship of the Scots.

During the short reign of Kenneth's brother Donald I the young kingdom was invaded by two Northumbrian princes, Osbrecht and Ella, along with Cumbrian Britons and a number of Picts who had taken refuge in England.

They advanced to Jedburgh where Donald was victorious, but a surprise attack at Berwick dispersed his army and made Donald a prisoner. The Northumbrians obtained a king's ransom – all the dominions south of the Forth plus whatever stronghold there was at Stirling, which they refortified and manned with a strong garrison. They also erected the first stone bridge over the Forth. The land to the west of the river was bog and the marshlands of Flanders, Blairdrummond and Drip Moss. These were drained in later centuries but long made Stirling Bridge the only practical place for armies to cross the Forth. A tale told of this time says that the Northumbrians were expecting an attack by invading Vikings. A sentry fell asleep but a wolf on the crag heard the Danes approaching and gave so many howls and growls that the sentry woke up and the garrison repulsed the invaders. Until 1975, when Stirling's burgh status was abolished at regionalisation, Stirling had a wolf crouching on a crag in its coat of arms to symbolise alertness and the need to keep the castle rock defended at all times. At the new millennium, Stirling marked the occasion by burning a giant effigy of a wolf, which shows the thanks you get sometimes!

Stirling's wolf. Wolves must have been fairly common at one time. There is a record from 1288 of payment for a wolf hunter and two park keepers at Stirling, presumably for the King's Park. Today, golf and football are more typical. Wolf Crag Quarry, in the Ochils near Bridge of Allan, is said to be the last haunt of the wolf in Scotland. The wolf story is still commemorated in an effigy on the council's Wolfcraig Buildings, one of the first structures in Scotland with steel-beam construction and electric lighting. (*Stirling Council*)

The remaining 200 years or so of the Alpin dynasty saw control of southern Scotland – including Stirling, Edinburgh and the Borders – pass back and forth between Alba and England, starting centuries of Anglo-Scottish rivalry that echoes even now, a thousand years later. In 973 Kenneth III mustered an army at Stirling, almost certainly his capital, to defeat a Danish invasion at Luncarty. In 1018 Malcolm II reinstated the full kingdom of Alba including Sutherland, Caithness, Lothian and Strathclyde, and the original border between Scotland and England that remains today. In gaining Lothian, Malcolm struck a bargain with the English that he would not change the traditions and language of the area. This entrenched the distinction – still in existence – between the Gaelic-speaking Highlanders and the Lowlanders who speak Scots. Malcolm II sired no sons so he named his grandson Duncan – son of his eldest daughter Bethoc and Crinan, Abbott of Dunkeld – to be king after his demise and then set about slaughtering all the male descendants of Kenneth III. Aged eighty when he died in 1034 after a reign of almost thirty years – both incredible for the time – Malcolm II ensured that Duncan I was proclaimed King of Alba, from the Tweed in the south to Moray in the north, a suitable send-off for the last Alpin monarch. MacBeth murdered Duncan in 1040, but Duncan's son Malcolm got his own back in 1057.

Scotland was now held by the Dunkeld dynasty, but would soon be receiving the attentions of the Normans. Although we know that Stirling Castle was used by King Malcolm III (Malcolm Canmore, husband of St Margaret) before 1096, its present incarnation dates from the twelfth century, when the town first received its charter as a royal burgh. The castle then would have had little in common with today's edifice. It would most likely have consisted of timber buildings surrounded by a palisaded rampart. Alexander I, Malcolm's fifth son and the third to become king, dedicated a chapel in the early 1100s and died there in 1124. His brother David I, who succeeded him, gave the town royal burgh status in 1124, making Stirling one of the most important towns of medieval Scotland.

A merchant guild was founded to administer the market and trading privileges granted by the king. The charters were issued partly out of royal self-interest – the king wanted to ensure a steady supply of craftsmen and merchants for his own buildings and the ready provision of cloth, candles and cooking pots, furniture, foods and wine and imports from afar. The Crown would also receive tithes, feus and duties from charters granted and preferments bestowed.

Stirling remained an important royal palace throughout the twelfth and thirteenth centuries. Possession of Stirling has therefore always been significant, over and above its status as a royal palace. In 1174, it was one of four Scottish castles surrendered to Henry II of England in return for the freedom of King William the Lion, captured in battle at Alnwick. It was returned to Scots control in 1189 and William died in the castle in 1214. The battles of Stirling Bridge in 1297 and Bannockburn in 1314 were fought nearby as England and Scotland vied for control of this significant area and its citadel.

William Wallace

> This is the truth I tell you:
> of all things freedom's most fine.
> Never submit to live, my son,
> in the bonds of slavery entwined.
>
> William Wallace – his uncle's proverb,
> from Bower's *Scotichronicon, c.* 1440s.

Wallace has had a lasting influence on Stirling. His battle of 1297, the monument that bears his name, innumerable statues erected in his memory and the iconic portrayal of him by Mel Gibson in the film *Braveheart* have planted Stirling in worldwide consciousness. We will never know how much of Wallace is man and how much is myth. His story comes to us mostly through Blind Harry's 1478 poem, 'The Wallace', which for centuries afterwards, until its last printing in 1859, was the second most popular book in Scotland after the Bible. Henry the Minstrel (usually called Blind Harry) collated his epic from a Latin narrative, written in about 1370 by John of Fordun, the *Orygnale Cronykil* of Andrew of Wyntoun written in 1420 and Walter Bower's *Scotichronicon*, written in the 1440s, and added a few embellishments. Composed at a time when mass printing was just becoming possible thanks to an Englishman called Caxton living in Bruges, 'The Wallace' became the most influential long poem ever written in Scots. By then, folk memory was already ascribing to Wallace powers he never had and events that he took no part in. At least two major episodes in the poem simply did not happen – English atrocities at the Barns of Ayr and Wallace's victory at Biggar – nor did Wallace besiege York and march as far south as St Albans, as Blind Harry claims. However, it is worth noting that Mallory's *Morte D'Arthur* had been printed some twenty years before and the story of William Tell was being circulated, so Scotland was ripe for a tale of its own superhero.

William Wallace from an engraving by J.C. Armytage (1820–97), well known for his historical and landscape works.

History is usually written by the victors while the vanquished can only cry 'no fair!' Therefore William Wallace drives a huge scar through medieval chronicles. To the Scots he was the archetypal Scottish martyr, unyielding in his commitment to Scotland's independence, while to English chroniclers he was a murderer and an outlaw, responsible for appalling barbarity and atrocities and above all a traitor.

Very little is known of Wallace's life before about 1297. He was the younger son of a Scottish knight and landowner, Sir Malcolm le Waleis, who held lands in Elderslie, near Paisley. The name means the 'Gaulish' or 'Welshman', suggesting he was descended from the many Norman knights invited into Scotland in the wake of Queen Margaret at the close of the eleventh century, or from Richard Wallace who had followed the Stewart family back to Scotland 100 years later, after MacBeth had driven them into exile, or because he was of the Welsh-speaking people of Strathclyde. (The Welsh had been invited to help a king of Strathclyde defend his lands and had settled – the Borders town of Peebles is a rendering of *pebyll*, the wigwams they lived in, or possibly from *pobl*, Welsh for 'people' and *lle*, 'a place'.)

Wallace was certainly educated – his letters show a knowledge of French and Latin – and possibly at Paisley Abbey by his uncle, a priest of Dunipace near Stirling. His uncle apparently told him:

> *Dico tibi verum, libertas est optima rerum.*
> *Nunquam servili sub nexu vivite, fili.*

> I tell you truly, freedom is the right thing.
> Never live in the bonds of servitude, my son.

It is also likely that William Wallace had some military experience, given his later generalship.

The Battle of Stirling Bridge

In 1296 Scotland was a vassal nation. There had been turmoil for ten years. The last Celtic king, Alexander III, had died in a riding accident and the heir to the throne, his granddaughter Margaret, Maid of Norway, had perished on her way back to Scotland. The uncertainty over the succession was used by Edward I of England as a prime opportunity to interfere in Scotland's affairs and, in his role as invited mediator, he fomented old rivalries and appointed the weak John Balliol as king against the claim of the Bruce family. Edward then forced various humiliations on Balliol which resulted in inevitable war, several Scottish raids on Carlisle and Northumberland and fierce retaliation. Edward took Berwick after two days of burning and killing and routed the Scots at Dunbar. Balliol surrendered his kingdom and went into captivity then exile. Edward, who by this time had seized the public archives and any historical monuments proving the antiquity and freedom of Scotland – including the

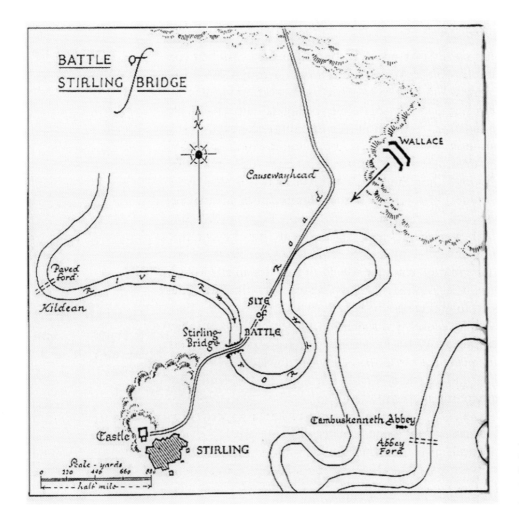

A map showing the key area of the Battle of Stirling Bridge. (*Courtesy of Pam Reitsch*)

Stone of Destiny on which the Kings of Scots were crowned – and had bribed many of the Scottish nobles with English lands and privileges, left Scotland in the hands of the Earl of Surrey, as if it were a province of England.

Deep resentments boiled. Many of the Scots were in prison or punitively taxed or pressed into service against France. Suddenly, Wallace leaps to the fore in an act of calculated revolt. In May 1297 he killed William Heselrig, the English Sheriff of Lanark. This uprising gained momentum, and from his base in the Ettrick Forest Wallace and his followers attacked Scone, Ancrum and Dundee. In the Black Isle to the north, Andrew Moray (or Murray) was at the head of an even more successful rising. He took Inverness, stormed Urquhart Castle on Loch Ness and cleared the north-east, while his Clan MacDougall allies harried the west and the rising drew support from the south. Most of Scotland was liberated, so Wallace and Moray now faced the prospect of open battle with the disciplined and well-armed English, recalled from their French campaigns and augmented by Welsh bowmen.

On 11 September 1297 Wallace and Moray won a decisive victory at Stirling Bridge, by the obvious if unanticipated ploy of waiting until part of the English and Welsh army had crossed the bridge, then demolishing it under them. The English attempted to attack early in the morning but were recalled because their commander, Warenne, had slept too late. Two Dominican friars were sent to demand Wallace's surrender but returned with his answer and first recorded speech: 'Tell your commander that we are not here to make peace but to do battle, defend ourselves and liberate our kingdom. Let them come on, and we shall prove this in their very beards.'

Encamped on the Abbey Craig, which would later be the site of the Wallace Monument, Wallace directed Stirling man John Wright to pull out a series of pins, causing the bridge to collapse. He was forever after known as 'Pin' Wright and the eldest son was thereafter given the nickname. The family kept alive the tradition for over 600 years, the last Pin Wright dying in 1900.

The English who had crossed to the north side had no room for manoeuvre and were massacred by Scottish spearmen, while those on the south side watched on helplessly. The English had 5,000 dead including the despised Hugh Cressingham whose flayed skin Wallace used to make a sword belt. Only one group of English knights, commanded by Sir Marmaduke Twenge, made their way back to the bridge. After they had crossed, Warenne, who had wisely stayed put, destroyed the bridge and fled to Berwick.

The only significant Scots casualty was Andrew Moray, who was badly wounded and died in the November. Notice, though, the absence of Robert Bruce, off pursuing his own interests in Irvine at the time, where he had been defeated and had offered surrender terms and a treaty to the English. Bruce seems to have been very confused as to where his loyalties lay, at least to begin with and he changed sides five times. By rights, his feudal superior was Edward I but in 1297 he sided with William Wallace, at least in spirit, and is quoted as saying 'No man holds his flesh and blood in hatred, and I am no exception. I must join my own people and the nation in whom I was born.' But a few months later he was back in the English camp.

THE STIRLING BRIDGES

Tourists are often shown Stirling Bridge as 'The place where William Wallace fought the Battle of Stirling Bridge'. That would have been a great feat requiring over 200 years of time travel. Before this bridge was built by James IV in about 1500 there were earlier structures, including the wooden bridge where Wallace did indeed defeat the English. This was the lowest bridging point over the River Forth for almost 400 years and its chief function was as a customs post to levy duties on goods entering the burgh. Excise collectors sat in a covered booth in the middle of the bridge. In 1571 a gallows was built on the bridge for the hanging of Archbishop Hamilton, scourge of the Protestant reformers. During the 1745 Jacobite rebellion the southern arch was blown up by General Blackney to prevent the Highlanders from entering Stirling and was not rebuilt until 1749. It is located off Drip Road a few hundred yards north of the town centre.

Stirling New Bridge was designed by Robert Stevenson (the famous author's grandfather) and opened in 1833. Alternative schemes by Thomas Telford were rejected. The Stevenson family of engineers was also involved in driving a channel up the Forth from Alloa, through the many fords that made river traffic uneconomic. Despite this – and because the railways arrived soon after – Stirling's time as a trading harbour all but came to an end.

The importance of the Forth as a barrier to Highland incursions is neatly given in Robert Louis Stevenson's novel *Kidnapped: The Adventures of David Balfour*. 'It's a chief principle in military affairs,' said he, 'to go where ye are least expected. Forth is our trouble; ye ken the saying, "Forth bridles the wild Hielandman." Well, if we seek to creep round about the head of that river and come down by Kippen or Balfron, it's just precisely there that they'll be looking to lay hands on us. But if we stave on straight to the auld Brig of Stirling, I'll lay my sword they let us pass unchallenged.'

Stirling Old Bridge from a postcard of the early 1900s. (*BD*)

Wallace later advanced against Northumberland and was knighted — possibly by Robert Bruce, who again managed to change sides more than once during this period — and anointed Commander of the Army of the Kingdom of Scotland and Guardian of Scotland in Balliol's name. This was a remarkable achievement — a mere knight wielding power over the nobles of a medieval Scotland obsessed with position and hierarchy. Wallace used his success not to garner personal power — he was offered the kingship but turned it down in favour of Balliol — but to influence Scottish national and international policy.

Stirling Bridge was the first battle in Europe where an army of common spearmen defeated a feudal horde. A mere five years later a host of French knights went down to similarly armed Flemish townsmen at the Battle of Courtrai. The engagement also destroyed the myth of English invincibility — the Scots had not been victorious on home soil since the Dark Ages — but their success merely strengthened the resolve of Edward Longshanks.

The Battle of Falkirk

Less than a year later, on 22 July 1298, the Scots army was defeated at the Battle of Falkirk by an army composed largely of Irish and Welsh infantry. Wallace had misjudged Edward's tactics and Welsh longbowmen were the decisive factor against the Scots spearmen. However, it should be said that Wallace's 30,000 were outnumbered almost three to one. He was also let down by Red Comyn, who felt he should have command, and by Robert Bruce, who was on the English side.

There is a tradition that Wallace and Bruce met for a parley after the battle. Bruce tried to persuade Wallace of the folly of his ways, but in the event it was Bruce whose mind was turned to thoughts of promoting a Scotland independent of England's overlordship. Whether this is the case or not, the English won the day, although Wallace took the edge off their victory. After his conference with Bruce he gathered up what was left of his army at Torwood and marched the half-dozen miles north to Stirling, burning the burgh and despoiling the countryside to deny the enemy provisions. Arriving at Perth, Wallace stepped down as Guardian of Scotland, to be replaced by the joint guardianship of Robert Bruce (who had, yet again, crucially failed to support Wallace) and his enemy Comyn. But Stirling was again in English hands.

Wallace, no longer with any authority in Scotland but now a renowned figure throughout Europe, was sent abroad as an envoy. In 1299 he attended the court of King Philip IV of France, was briefly imprisoned for various political reasons but soon released and given safe conduct to the Papal court. He proclaimed Scotland's renewed independence (he had already written offering trading links to the mayors of Hamburg and Lübeck, whose treaty of 1241 had laid the foundations of the Hanseatic League) and he persuaded the Pope to appoint the patriot Bishop Lamberton to the vacant bishopric of St Andrews, as a neutral third guardian to maintain order between Bruce and Comyn.

The Scots laid siege to the castle at Stirling and recaptured it in 1299. The English constable, John Sampson, was forced to surrender when a promised relief force failed to arrive. By 1303 Stirling was the only major Scottish stronghold to remain in Scottish hands, making Edward all the more determined to take it. He used floating bridges to cross the Forth below Stirling and established himself at Dunfermline. There he set about building the great siege engines, including a stone-throwing machine he called his 'War Wolf'. The siege began in April 1304, and on 20 July Sir William Oliphant offered the castle's surrender. But that wasn't nearly good enough for the 'Hammer of the Scots'. Edward insisted on part of the garrison remaining inside until he had tried out his 'War Wolf'.

Wallace had returned to Scotland in 1301, seemingly with the diplomatic high ground. However, the French needed Edward's help to suppress Flanders and abandoned the Scots. Bruce defected to Edward's cause, even attending the English Parliament in 1302. Panicking, the Scottish nobles again did fealty to Edward. Only Wallace refused to submit, thereby signing his own death warrant. He had become a nuisance to both nations. Robert Bruce again switched sides a few times during this period, always fearing that Comyn would gain ascendancy.

Wallace's small force was defeated by an army of English knights at Happrew, near Peebles. Wallace survived, but became a fugitive. Edward destroyed the monastery at Dunfermline in retribution for the rebellious parliaments held there and records were purposely burned or removed to London, destroying the evidence of Scotland's independence and a great deal of its history. He then laid siege to Stirling Castle, the last major fortification to resist his army.

Wallace's Martyrdom

Wallace was declared an outlaw, which meant his life was forfeit without trial. Although he continued his resistance, he was captured at Robroyston, near Glasgow on 3 August 1305 by Sir John Menteith, while travelling to meet the treacherous Robert Bruce. Although 'false' Menteith has gone down in Scottish legend as a traitor – Lake Menteith is the only 'lake' in Scotland as no betrayer of Wallace could have a 'loch' – he merely did what many others would have done, including, at the time, Robert Bruce. As proof, we have Menteith's seal on the 1320 Declaration of Arbroath, which was effectively Scotland's Bill of Rights and Declaration of Independence.

Wallace was taken captive to Dumbarton Castle, but was moved to London for a show trial in Westminster, charged with being an outlaw and a traitor. Edward knew that no trial was necessary but wanted to destroy his reputation. Wallace was not allowed to be represented or to speak, but when accused of being a traitor, he denied it saying that he had never been Edward's subject to begin with. Inevitably he was found guilty, wrapped in ox hide to prevent him being ripped apart as he was dragged by horses 4 miles through London to Smithfield, hanged as a murderer and thief, but cut down while still alive, disembowelled and emasculated. For the crime of sacrilege against English monasteries his heart, lungs, liver and entrails were cast onto a fire, and, finally, his head was cut off and set on a pole on London Bridge. His body was quartered and sent to Newcastle (which Wallace had destroyed in 1297–8), Berwick, Perth and Stirling, as a warning to the Scots.

Opposite: Brechin sculptor Tom Church underwent open heart surgery in May 1995. In the aftermath, at a physical and spiritual low, he saw the film *Braveheart* featuring Mel Gibson and was inspired to capture its mood in stone. From January 1996 he worked for over 1,000 hours on 2 blocks of sandstone, each weighing 6 tons, and finished the sculpture on 11 May, a year to the day since his operation. It found its natural home at the base of Abbey Craig and was unveiled by Nigel Tranter on 11 September 1997. (NP)

This was Edward's greatest mistake and Wallace's final victory – Edward had destroyed the man, but created the martyr. He would have done better leaving him to rot in prison. Wallace became the symbol of Scotland's freedom and entered the realm of myth, folktale, legend and Hollywood.

Robert Bruce and Bannockburn

Stirling Castle remained under English control until 1314. Edward I had died at Carlisle in 1307 and this, in combination with the coronation of Robert Bruce the previous year, gave the Scots new heart. By 1313 only four Scottish castles – Berwick, Bothwell, Edinburgh and Stirling – were under English control. Edward Bruce, Robert's younger brother, laid siege to Stirling. Sir Philip Moubray agreed that the castle would be handed over to the Scots if a relief force had not arrived by Midsummer's Day 1314. Edward II fell for this and crossed the River Tweed on 17 June with 20,000 men. He was met six days later at Bannockburn, just south of Stirling, by King Robert Bruce's army of 7,000. A number of factors are said to have contributed to the Scottish victory at Bannockburn. There was Bruce's own personal valour in killing Edward's champion single-handed, or, as some believe, the timely intervention of Knights Templar then sanctuaried in Scotland. Or perhaps it was the fact that Bruce's army carried before them holy relics, possibly a bone of St Columba, in the Monymusk reliquary. Or was it simply because the Scots had had enough of English incursions and fought their hearts out? Robert Bruce had pulled off one of Scotland's greatest victories (sometimes referred to, only half-jokingly, as 'our last home win'). Only Berwick remains in English hands to this day. This is one reason that dating Stirling Castle's original

'Let Scotland's warcraft be this: footsoldiers, mountains and marshy ground; and let her woods, her bow and spear serve for barricades. Let menace lurk in all her narrow places among her warrior bands, and let her plains so burn with fire that her enemies flee away. Crying out in the night, let her men be on their guard, and her enemies in confusion will flee from hunger's sword. Surely it will be so, as we're guided by Robert, our lord.' Ascribed to Robert Bruce in 1308 by Walter Bower in his continuation of John Fordun's *Scotichronicon*, *c.* 1440. This image is from a 1920s postcard of Robert Bruce's statue in Stirling Castle. (*BD*)

foundations is difficult – after Bannockburn Robert Bruce had the castle (or at least its fortifications) destroyed to deny it to the English in future.

Who was Robert Bruce?

It is easy to be taken in by the superficial myth of Robert Bruce, Earl of Carrick, warrior-king and liberator of the Scots. Deeper probing shows him to have been a self-serving opportunist whose loyalties were frequently swayed one way and then the other. Even his marriages were probably politically inspired. The first to Isabella, daughter of the Earl of Mar (overlord of the lands on which Stirling Castle stood and therefore a man of some importance), produced Marjory, mother of Robert II, later the first Stewart or Stuart king. His second marriage to Elizabeth, daughter of the Red Earl (Aylmer de Burgh, Earl of Ulster), was certainly inspired by a desire to consolidate his loyalty (at the time) to Edward I but may also have been intended to provide him with a foothold in Ireland and a way to the High Kingship. She also gave him a son, David II, who succeeded him.

Bruce came from a Norman French family from Brix in Flanders. In 1124, King David I granted large estates in Annandale to his supporter Robert de Brus in order to help secure the border. Born in 1274, Robert was the son of another Robert Bruce and grandson of yet another Robert Bruce, a failed claimant of the Scottish Crown in 1290–2. His mother, Marjorie, Countess of Carrick, brought him a lineage from Gaelic earls. She was quite an influential figure herself – she had apparently imprisoned Bruce's father on his return from the Crusades and refused to free him until he married her. The young Robert, brought up at Turnberry Castle, must have learned a great deal from her, including Gaelic, Scots and Norman French, and in addition his family's entitlement to the Crown of Scotland. In 1295, when he became Earl of Carrick, he was in a position to do something about it.

Initially, both Robert and his father supported Edward I's invasion of Scotland in 1296, hoping to gain the Crown after Balliol's imprisonment and exile. When Edward simply installed himself as king, they were bitterly disappointed. The next year, while Wallace was battling at Stirling Bridge, the Bruces were raising a failed revolt at Irvine. Rather than join with Wallace to help consolidate the Scottish victory, Bruce sought surrender terms and kept a low profile until he could judge the English reaction, although he is credited with a stirring speech before switching sides again. He was also absent from the Battle of Falkirk, at a time when his presence might have prevented Wallace's army from defeat and devastation. He used the opportunity of Wallace losing or resigning the Guardianship of Scotland in 1298 to have himself and John Comyn appointed jointly. 'Red' Comyn (so called on account of his hair and complexion) supported Balliol's claim to the throne, and Bruce was removed from office a year later. When it seemed Balliol might return, Bruce once again kowtowed to the English, hoping to have his claim recognised and quite prepared to rule as a vassal king.

To be fair, switching sides in pursuit of a personal goal was almost a national sport among the Scots nobles of the time. But Bruce's well-known oscillations may have been what prompted the composers of the Declaration of Arbroath some twenty years later to include the line: 'For as long as a hundred of us remain alive, we shall never on any conditions be subjected to the lordship of the English.'

For Robert Bruce 1304 was a crucial year. His father's death made him the claimant to the throne, and the collapse of the Scots in the face of English aggression ended all hopes of Balliol's restoration. Edward I had at last subjugated Scotland. But he was soon to die, and knowing that Edward II wasn't half the man his father had been, Bruce started to make alliances. In this year it appears that Bruce was coming round to the Scottish cause once and for all. He made the Bond of Cambuskenneth with Bishop Lamberton of St Andrews, the head of the Scottish Church. This was an important but typically shrewd move – if he made claim to the throne then the backing of the Church was important and this bond would help. However, there was still the opposing claim of the Comyns to deal with.

On 11 February 1306 Bruce met Red Comyn at Greyfriars Kirk in Dumfries, in theory a holy sanctuary and therefore safe ground for both. Bruce provoked an argument, swords were drawn, and Comyn was stabbed in front of the high altar. The murder may not have been premeditated, but it got Bruce excommunicated and outlawed, while Scotland disintegrated into a civil war. Bruce realised that the time for diplomacy and vacillation was over and the only path open to him was an uprising. Within six weeks his supporter Bishop Wishart had given him absolution and on 25 March 1306 he was hurriedly crowned at Scone by the Countess of Buchan (rather than the Earl of Fife, whose traditional and legal responsibility it was). He was not in any sense the people's hero at this juncture – few nobles or bishops had attended his coronation and he probably threatened many of his countrymen into giving their support.

The beginning of Bruce's reign was far from happy. Not only had he caused civil war as well as hostilities with England, one of his brothers, Neil, was hung, drawn and executed at Berwick and his sisters, wife and daughter imprisoned. His own forces were less than organised and in June they were defeated at Methven. Bruce fled to his Gaelic homeland in the west, hiding on Rathlin Island (off the Irish coast) and in the Hebrides. It is here that the legends begin to take over – the dispossessed king, hiding in caves, enduring all hardships for the good of his people and talking to spiders.

Fortunately, Bruce discovered that he was better as a guerrilla commander than a field warfare general and he achieved small but significant victories at Glen Trool and Loudon Hill. In 1308 he defeated the Comyns at Inverurie – possibly near Mons Graupius where the Romans had massacred the Caledonians more than 1,200 years before – and took Aberdeen. He then had control over the whole of Scotland north of Dundee and Perth. Acquiring Stirling was the obvious next step, but a rather large one.

The common folk started to realise that Bruce was their only hope against the tyranny of English rule, and by cold-bloodedly suppressing and exiling his opponents and rewarding those who joined him, he started to turn the tide.

He was also lucky in that Edward I, apoplectic with rage and intent on crushing the Scots once and for all, died on the march north within sight of the border. His successor, Edward II, sought a two-year truce, a misjudgement his father would never have made as it allowed Bruce time to marshal his forces and to give the Balliol faction an ultimatum – join the cause or forfeit their estates. By 1313 many had chosen Bruce.

Bruce now started to raid the remaining English strongholds. He had set his brother Edward to lay siege to Stirling. Sir James Douglas led a surprise assault on Roxburgh Castle which encouraged Thomas, Earl of Moray, to take Edinburgh Castle in a sneak attack. Edward had no choice but to confront Bruce on his own turf, and so in 1314 he led a massive army to meet the 30,000 Scots at Bannockburn. There is still controversy and confusion over the exact location of the battle. Much of the probable site is now covered by Bannockburn village, so historians have sited it on the flat land to the north next to the River Forth, and most paintings reflect this. However, in the fourteenth century this was not the flat fields we see today but a 'carse' – wet marsh of the flood plain. Even the incompetent Edward II would hardly have chosen to fight a battle on such ground. More likely, the battle took place on flatter land to the north of Bannockburn gorge. The point is, the choice of ground was Bruce's and he had selected it well. The banks of the small stream of the Bannock were steep and rugged and there were several small hillocks the Scots could occupy, giving themselves the advantage.

This print of the field of Bannockburn, drawn by D.O. Hill and engraved by W. Richardson, dates from the 1870s. Stirling and its castle can be seen some 3 miles to the north and beyond that Dumyat and the Ochils and the River Devon. (BD)

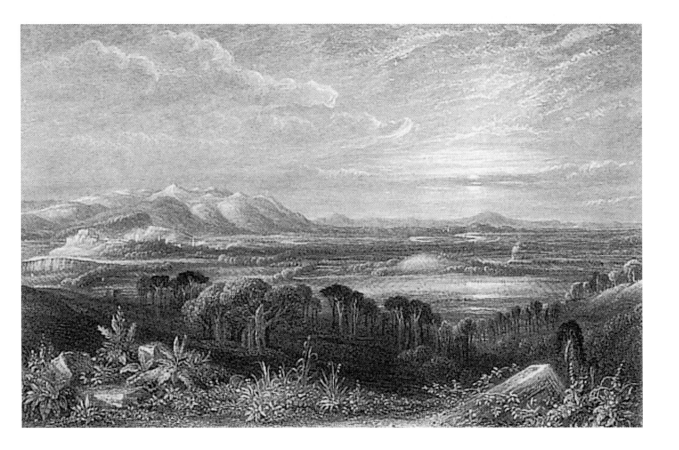

However, Stirling Castle was still in English hands, despite a long siege by Edward Bruce, Robert's brother, the spring before. But he had concluded a treaty with the governor, Philip Moubray, that if the garrison were not relieved by St John the Baptist's Day, 24 June, they should surrender. Robert was unhappy with this but confirmed it to save his brother's honour.

The date was auspicious because it had obliged Edward II to march on Scotland in order to beat the deadline. John de St John hoped to surprise the Scots by a forced march with 15,000 horse. But Edward Bruce was forewarned and ordered his infantry to entrench themselves in narrow ground. With only fifty horsemen, he attacked under cover of a thick mist, surprised the English on their march and dispersed them.

A body of 800 English cavalry was sent to the relief of Stirling Castle. Robert Bruce himself was the first to see them pass and sent the Earl of Moray to pursue them with 500 infantry. On the plain where the village of Newhouse now stands, a circle of spearsmen was attacked and surrounded. But the English were entirely defeated, with the loss of only one Scot. Two large stones, erected in the field as a commemoration, can still be seen in the village, about a quarter of a mile from the old South Port of Stirling. This victory raised the spirits of the Scots army and gave them encouragement for the general engagement the following day.

Edward, enraged at the defeat of his cavalry and conscious of the impact it would have on the morale of the rest of his army, resolved to bring it to an end the next day. But the Scots had the advantage of ground along the slope of a gentle hill about a mile south of Stirling Castle. On the right was a range of rocks, in front were the steep banks of the Bannock Burn, to the left was a bog and the English had the sun in their eyes. Bruce had also ordered pits dug in the morass and in the fields to the left, covered with green turf supported on stakes so as to look like firm ground and had sharp calthorps scattered around. Bruce is also credited with inventing the offensive–defensive technique known as the shiltrom – ranks of men armed with long pikes, advancing rank over rank like a lethal hedgehog – which was almost impenetrable to infantry and cavalry alike.

The front rank of the Scottish army stretched for a mile along the riverbank and two other detachments occupied the high ground on the right, commanded by Edward Bruce, and the low ground on the left under Bruce's nephew and greatest general, Sir Thomas Randolph, 1st Earl of Moray. (Just before Bannockburn, Randolph had recaptured Edinburgh Castle from the English by climbing its walls under cover of night. He was later named Regent to the young King David II, Bruce's son. His daughter, Black Agnes, wife of Patrick Earl of Dunbar, later became famous in her own right when she saw off a six-month siege on Dunbar Castle by the Earl of Salisbury in 1338, in the absence of her husband.)

Robert himself took charge of the centre and a fourth division was under Walter, Lord High Steward, and Sir James Douglas, both of whom had been knighted that morning. The enemy approached in three bodies led by the English king in person and by the Earls of Hereford and Gloucester, the best generals in England. Their centre was infantry and the wings cavalry. Archers were also placed at the wings and at intervals along the front. Edward was surprised that the Scots would face his formidable army. But when Sir Ingram Umfraville suggested a mock retreat to behind their tents – to tempt the Scots to plunder, so the English could turn and attack them – Edward rejected the idea. Surely there was no need for subtlety in dealing with such a small rabble.

The English cavalry charged Randolph's left wing, near where the bridge now stands in the village of Chartershall, the only place where the river could be crossed. Another detachment circled round to the flank and rear, but hit the barrier of sharp spikes and pits. Randolph took advantage of the disorder and charged. Edward's archers were pinned at the back of his other forces, unable to fire for fear of hitting their own men.

Meanwhile, an event took place which, though minor in itself, may have turned the battle. Robert was riding before his lines, carrying only a battle-axe and wearing a crown on his helmet so he could be recognised. An English knight, Sir Henry de Boun, galloped up to engage Bruce in single combat, expecting to end the contest and gain fame for his chivalry. But he missed his strike and was instantly killed by Bruce's axe which cleaved his helmet to the neck and suffered a broken handle with the force of the impact. The Scots rushed the enemy, supported by 500 cavalry. English cavalry charged the right wing of Edward Bruce but Randolph marched to his aid. There was no clear advantage to either side, but another event turned it to the Scot's favour.

The famous statue of Robert Bruce at Bannockburn was unveiled by Queen Elizabeth in 1964. (*Stirling Council*)

Whether this was a spontaneous display of patriotic fervour or a premeditated tactic, 15,000 'sma' folk' – ghillies, servants and attendants who had taken the baggage behind an adjoining hill – suddenly marched to the top. Waving white sheets on long poles in place of banners, they rushed towards the English who panicked and scattered, with Edward last to leave the field. The hill is now known as Gillies Hill in their honour, despite the change in spelling.

It is also said that Knights Templar fought at Bruce's side and possibly led the charge of the 'sma' folk'. Certainly there were Templars in Scotland at that time – their Grand Master Hugues de Payen had visited Scotland in 1128–9, Bruce had offered them a safe haven after the dissolution of their order in 1312 and St John's Day had special significance in the Templar calendar. It may also be relevant that Edward subsequently confiscated all Templar properties in England in 1315, possibly in retribution.

The Scots pursued and slaughtered the enemy, especially as they tried to cross the river. Some drowned attempting the Forth and some headed for the safety of Stirling Castle. The Earl of Hereford retreated to Bothwell where the castle was garrisoned by the English, but he had no choice but to surrender and was later exchanged for Robert's wife and daughter, and other supporters who had been held captive for eight years in England.

King Edward rode to Stirling Castle but was told that it could not be defended, so he headed south accompanied by a scant fifteen nobles and a small body of cavalry. He was pursued for more than 40 miles by Sir James Douglas who almost caught him, causing the English king to make a vow that should he escape, he would build and endow a religious house in Oxford. (In 1326 he founded Oriel, Oxford's fifth oldest college.) He reached Dunbar Castle in time and although Douglas waited a few days, hoping to catch him trying to escape on land, he was smuggled away by sea in a fishing boat.

Bruce then made use of what we would today call a publicity stunt – or rather, three. First, when Stirling Castle surrendered the next day, the garrison was allowed to leave unharmed. Moubray was so impressed by this chivalry that he offered his services. It also meant, of course, he kept his house and possessions. Second, equally well treated was an old friend of Robert's, Sir Marmaduke Twenge, who had narrowly escaped death at Stirling Bridge all those years before. When he gave himself up he was treated with great civility and sent home not only without ransom, but loaded with presents. This was good public relations on Bruce's part, but he showed less consideration to his own countrymen who did not return to his allegiance after the battle. Third, Bruce had the history written in his favour.

Edward had been so confident of obliterating the Scots that he had brought the laureated bard and Carmelite monk Andrew Baston to write a celebration. Baston had gone with Edward I to Scotland in 1304 in the same capacity and had written 'De Strivilniensi Obsidione' ('The Siege of Stirling Castle'), 'De Altero Scotorum' and other poems. This time, by way of ransom, he was ordered to compose a poem in praise of the Scots' victory. While he did so with fairly bad grace, he did confirm many of the historical facts and a list of the most important English killed in battle.

Bannockburn established Robert firmly on the throne and settled a much-needed calm on the country. But often the greatest consequences of victory are economic. The extensive Balliol possessions and those of his followers were forfeit and gave the king even greater power. He kept some of these estates for himself and bestowed the rest on his friends, who became even more strongly attached to his cause. The rich plunder in the English camp – money, armour, sumptuous furniture, plate, rich clothes, ornaments – and ransom paid by prisoners of rank increased the national wealth and provided a greater circulation of money in Scotland than it had ever seen. The results were soon visible – large mansions were built, there was time and peace to plan more elegant houses and gardens and the commoners could exchange their swords for ploughshares and pay attention to agriculture. It also upset English plans for the domination, not only of Scotland, but also of France, and so affected the destiny of Europe.

The popular picture of Robert Bruce is not completely at odds with history – outnumbered, fighting valiantly for Scotland's independence against superior English forces, engaging the English champion and winning, just as Wallace had done at Stirling Bridge seventeen years earlier, and afterwards establishing a peaceful and prosperous rule. But it is worth recalling that he did it mostly for himself, not his subjects. Now in total control of Scotland, however, he still had not achieved his main aim – Scotland's independence and his own monarchy recognised by the English, the Pope and Christendom as a whole.

Capitalising on the English humiliation and Gaelic sentiment, Bruce opened up a second front when he dispatched his brother to invade Ireland in 1315. Edward Bruce also had a reasonable claim to the Irish High Kingship and was supported by Ireland's most powerful king, Domnall Ua Neill, a kinsman through the Bruce's maternal grandfather. However, as often seems to be the case with campaigns in Ireland, it was a disaster. Famine blighted the land and Edward Bruce was killed in 1318. The whole exercise could be seen as device to force the English to fight on two fronts and, hence, take the heat off Scotland, or it could have been just another example of the Bruce family's vaulting ambition. Had Edward Bruce ruled Ireland, would they have stopped there? Or tried their hand in Wales, Northumbria and even England as a whole? Later events suggest this to be more than likely.

On the diplomatic front, the Scots constructed the Declaration of Arbroath in 1320, an assertion of Scotland's independence and maturity as a self-governing people, a Bill of Rights and a Magna Carta all rolled into one. It was to no avail. The Pope ignored it and the English were hardly in any mood to take it seriously. Bruce accepted a truce with Edward II, but after the latter's murder by his wife and her lover, Roger Mortimer, Edward III was crowned at only sixteen years old. Seizing the moment, Bruce launched an invasion of northern England, threatening to annex it to Scotland. Edward III's government was forced to recognise Bruce's kingship and Scotland's independence. A year later, in 1329, Bruce died of leprosy, his ambitions finally realised.

Bruce's body is buried in Dunfermline Abbey. His heart, sent on a crusade as he requested, is buried at Melrose Abbey with the inscription: 'A noble hart may haiff nane es . . . Gyff fredome failyhe' – 'A noble heart has no ease . . . if freedom fail', from *Bruce* by John Barbour (1320–95).

The Castle Lost and Regained

But Bruce's hard-won victories and independence were relatively short-lived. Realising its strategic significance, Edward III of England had Stirling Castle rebuilt and strengthened between 1333 and 1336 after his victory at Halidon Hill in support of the puppet 'king' Edward Balliol, son of John, who had sailed an English fleet to Fife, marched to Scone and had himself crowned in 1332. The English garrison, captained by Sir Thomas Rokeby, was besieged in 1337 by Andrew Moray (the son of Wallace's ally). But it was not until the reign of David II in 1342 that it was recaptured by Robert the Steward, who later succeeded David II as King of Scots.

David II, son by a second marriage and successor of Robert Bruce, recovered the castle. However, David was taken prisoner at the Battle of Neville's Cross, near Durham in 1346, conveyed to the Tower of London and did not recover his liberty for eleven years. His nephew, Robert (later Robert II), ruled as regent. David was released in 1357 as part of the Treaty of Berwick, on promising to pay a heavy ransom – 100,000 merks – in annual instalments. This was a substantial sum at any time, but especially so when a third of his subjects had been wiped out by the Black Death in 1348. In 1363, after the death of Princess Joan of England, Edward III's daughter, he offered instead to leave the Scottish Crown to an English heir but his nobles opposed this and the Scottish Parliament threw out the very idea of a Union of the Crowns. He died in 1371, without either of his wives producing an heir, thus paving the way for his nephew Robert the Steward (Robert Bruce's grandson) to become Robert II and the first Stewart king.

The Borestone at Bannockburn, which so inspired Robert Burns to write 'Scots Wha' Hae'. The hut and the aged retainer in this early twentieth-century photograph are no longer there. The pillar was erected by Oddfellows of Stirling and Dumbarton in 1870. (*SCLS*)

3

The Coming of the Stewarts

Robert Bruce's victory was short-lived. His successor David II spent most of his reign in prison or in hock to the English. By 1336 Stirling Castle was back in English hands, held by Sir Thomas Rokeby who carried out rebuilding and strengthening work. Andrew Moray, son of Wallace's fellow general, laid siege to the castle in 1337 but failed to take it. Five years later Bruce's grandson Robert the Steward took it, which is the origin of the Stewart, or Stuart, dynasty. He succeeded David II as Robert II, King of Scots in 1371. Robert gave up trying in 1384 and handed the reins of power to his son John who took the title Robert II. Scotland descended into anarchy. Very little happened to the castle at Stirling during these years save the construction of the north gate, although a fire in 1405 almost completely destroyed the town.

James I and II – The Castle Takes Shape

The present buildings of Stirling Castle date mainly from the fifteenth and sixteenth centuries during which time it was the main royal palace outside the capital. It is hard to imagine a more unfortunate dynasty than the Stewarts. They had their share of bad luck, but they brought most of it on themselves. Of the six immediate predecessors of James VI all ascended the throne before their majority (two were mere infants) and all suffered unnatural deaths. Generally, their reigns were disastrous for themselves and the nation.

James I spent eighteen years in English captivity. On his return in 1424 he granted Stirling Castle to his English queen Joan as part of her marriage settlement. James was vindictive and murderous and blamed his uncle, Robert Stewart, Duke of Albany, governor in his absence, for not freeing him. Robert had died at Stirling Castle four years before so James charged his son, Murdoch, with his father's crime. On 24 May 1425 a parliament found against Murdoch so he, two of his sons and his father-in-law, the eighty-year-old Earl of Lennox, were executed on the Heading (or Beheading) Stone on nearby Gowan Hill. This was the first state execution for over 100 years and it probably did not escape the king's attention that as a result he recovered three major earldoms with an income of over £1,000 a year.

Eventually, the exasperated nobles, led by the Earl of Atholl, had James killed in his bed at his apartments in the Dominican friary at Perth on 20 February 1437. No coup as such took place. His seven-year-old son, a surviving twin, succeeded him as James II. Two years later, after her second marriage, Queen Joan was effectively imprisoned in her own castle of Stirling. However, the episode had another lasting effect – Dunfermline was deemed too unsafe to be the capital, which was moved to Edinburgh. Stirling, along with Scone, Perth and other residences, retained royal palace status.

Stirling was soon to see another murder borne out of kingly rage, which tradition says took place in the King's Old Building but as this had not been built at the time it may have happened in an earlier building on the same site. In 1452 James invited William the 8th Earl of Douglas to a dinner at Stirling Castle, guaranteeing him safe passage. Douglas refused to give up certain alliances and the king, unable to contain his anger, stabbed Douglas twenty-nine times, the royal bodyguard finishing him off and throwing his body from a window. This act of base treachery outraged the whole nation and James commanded little respect thereafter. James was enthusiastic about arms, commissioning and acquiring massive cannon such as Mons Meg (which can still be seen at Edinburgh Castle), and fortifying Stirling. It was probably a relief to everyone when, in 1460, James was killed by an accidental explosion of one of his beloved cannon. The eldest of his four sons succeeded him as James III.

James III – Great Builder, Poor King

James III was born in Stirling Castle in 1452, the same year as James II, his father, began his feud with the 'Black Douglases'. Disfigured by a birthmark,

The Heading (or Beheading) Stone on Gowan Hill is said to have been used for executions in the fifteenth century, including those of various important persons. (*BD*)

which earned him the nickname 'Fiery Face', James was only seven when his father was killed and two years later he had to be smuggled out of Edinburgh Castle to Stirling in a trunk to avoid being taken hostage or worse. For years he was a pawn in other people's power battles. In 1440, aged ten, he was the nominal host of what came to be known as the 'Black Dinner', organised by his 'tutor' Crichton, at which the teenage Earl of Douglas and his younger brother were taken outside Stirling Castle and beheaded.

But in James III at last Stirling had a king willing to take it seriously. His works included the castle walls, an unidentified 'white tower' in 1463 and major alterations to the chapel between 1467 and 1469. Some people believe that the Great Hall or Parliament Hall was his work, but it is now generally thought that this was more likely to have been the work of his son, James IV. However, James III's weakness and inability to learn from mistakes dogged him further. His own son was forced to lead a rebellion against him in 1488, culminating in the Battle of Sauchieburn.

The king was kept from occupying Stirling Castle by Governor Shaw, who was of the other persuasion. The armies met on the eastern side of the Sauchie Burn, 2 miles south of Stirling and a scant mile from Bannockburn. When the action became hand-to-hand, James forsook any courage he had found and sped off to board a ship. But just as he was crossing the Bannock Burn near Beaton's Mill in the village of Milton, James was thrown from the saddle and was concussed. The miller and his wife carried the fallen rider to their home. Convinced he was dying, James asked that a priest be called and announced to his stunned hosts: 'I was your king this morning.'

The Douglas Room where James II perpetrated one of the greatest acts of treachery of any Scottish monarch in February 1452. He murdered Black Douglas and threw him from the window. This room is now part of the Argyll and Sutherland Highlanders Museum but was then one of the royal apartments. (*BD*)

The poor miller's wife ran outside, wringing her hands, and calling for someone to help the king. This was something of a misjudgement as tradition tells that one of the rebel army passing heard her and answered that he was a priest. He heard the king's confession then promptly stabbed him to death. When James III died, nobody mourned him much. When his corpse was eventually found it was carried to Stirling Castle where it lay in state until interred in Cambuskenneth Abbey.

When the royalist army heard of the king's death, they fell back to Stirling. They were not pursued and the battle ceased. The army of the rebels marched to Linlithgow the next day. 'The field of Stirling', now better known as the Battle of Sauchieburn was over. His queen Margaret, daughter of Christian I of Norway and Denmark, spent the last three years of her life in Stirling Castle, a virtual prisoner. As for his son James IV, he wore ever after an iron chain next to his skin, adding a link every year as a penance for the unnatural acts of parricide and regicide against a father he had no reason to love.

James III added substantially to Stirling Castle, more so than his father had. His commissioned work included the castle walls, an unidentified White Tower in 1463, and major rebuilding in the chapel from 1467 to 1469. It is often said that the Great Hall or Parliament Hall was his work but it is now thought more likely to have been due to his son James IV. (*Stirling Council*)

James IV – Castle Builder

James IV, born in 1473, ruled from 1488 to 1513, and was possibly the first worthy king Scotland had had since David I, 'the Saint'. James IV was a great builder, especially at Stirling Castle where it is likely that the Great Hall, the King's Old Building (1500) and the gatehouse (1510) were commissioned by

him, as well as Stirling Old Bridge, the stone structure replacing the wooden one. Fond of his mother Margaret of Denmark, he had stayed with her in Stirling Castle and remained there after her death in 1486 until he was persuaded to join the nobles who had risen against James III culminating in the Battle of Sauchieburn.

This James was everything his father hadn't been – energetic, manly, open-minded, brave, courteous and genuinely interested in his realm and subjects. Everywhere he went he inspired loyalty and confidence, even among the Highland chiefs and especially women he met. Under his influence, his court became the most glamorous it had ever been or would be again. The great scholar Erasmus commented of James that he had wonderful powers of mind and an astonishing knowledge. The king spoke French, Flemish, German, Italian and Spanish, as well as Latin (the international language of the time) and even took the trouble to learn some Gaelic. His interest in literature, architecture, science and the law was well known and he even tried his hand at minor surgery and dentistry. James IV's reign was truly a Scottish renaissance. He stimulated the growth of learning, supported the universities (including founding Aberdeen), helped establish Scotland's first printing press under Andrew Myllar in Edinburgh, laid the foundation for Scotland's liberal and compulsory education system, supported a College of Surgeons and built up the navy. He brought Robert Carver, possibly Scotland's finest ever composer, to the Chapel Royal at Stirling.

The king's interest in all things scientific is possibly what caused the French (or Italian) alchemist John Damian, last Abbot of Tongland, to attempt to fly

The Great Hall, the King's Old Building and the gatehouse probably all date from James IV's reign. Other building and rebuilding works of his time include Linlithgow Palace, Edinburgh Castle, Falkland Palace, Holyrood and Rothesay. James was more apt to build ships and palaces than monasteries or churches and was little concerned with pleasing the clergy. He had an illegitimate son made an archbishop at eleven years old. (*BD*)

CAMBUSKENNETH

Situated a mile south of Abbey Craig and the Wallace Monument, Cambuskenneth may have been named after Kenneth MacAlpin who defeated the Picts at the Battle of Logie in the ninth century. The first mention of Cambuskenneth in local records is a charter by King David I dated 1140. In a later charter (1147) he granted to the Church the lands of Cambuskenneth and the fishing there, at Polmaise and other places, a tithe of the produce from one ship and a salt pit. In 1709 Cambuskenneth and Craigton were purchased by a trust for the sum of £61,972 Scots. Before that, Cambuskenneth was in the county of Clackmannan.

Cambuskenneth was known for its produce. The monks were proficient in horticulture and Cambuskenneth was long famous for its apples. The Cambuskenneth Red is still a popular variety in the USA, although the last apple trees in the village were removed in the 1960s.

The remains of Cambuskenneth Abbey lie between the castle and the Abbey Craig, on a fertile carse within a bend of the River Forth. Originally called the Abbey of St Mary, the Augustinian house was founded by King David I in 1147, was visited by King Edward I of England in 1303–4 during one of his numerous invasions of Scotland and was closely involved with the Battle of Bannockburn in 1314. The meeting of Bruce's First Parliament was held here in 1326, the first to include representatives from Scotland's burgh, but whose main purpose was to confirm that Bruce's son would become King David II. James III married Margaret, Princess of Denmark, in 1467. As part of the dowry, Scotland acquired the Orkneys in 1468 and Shetland the next year, providing substantial and much-needed revenues to the Crown, especially in terms of the fishing rights. But he also managed to lose Berwick-upon-Tweed to the English, so settling the Scottish border where it has been ever since. James III and his queen were buried in the grounds, but the exact location of their graves was lost until 1864 when a local legend turned out to be correct – that the royal couple had been buried near a hawthorn tree that had grown where the high altar had been. Their tomb was moved and made more suitable for royal personages by order of Queen Victoria in 1865.

Cambuskenneth Abbey and the tomb of James III and Margaret of Denmark, seen here in the early twentieth century. (*SCLS*)

The late Georgian and early Victorian village of Cambuskenneth is centred on South and North Streets. The ferry, which was in almost daily use since 1140, finished its service when the Cambuskenneth Bridge was built in the early 1900s as a work scheme for the unemployed. The village expanded slowly over the years as the trust that had owned it since 1709 released areas of ground for development. Cambuskenneth, Abbey Craig and Craigton only came under the jurisdiction of Stirling burgh in 1939. (*SCLS*)

The monastery at Cambuskenneth and the burgh of Stirling co-existed uneasily for centuries. Cambuskenneth was outwith the jurisdiction of the burgh council and in another county (Clackmannanshire) and benefited from the bounty of the Forth. On 26 July 1530, according to the abbot, the provost and Council of Stirling had ruffians attack the net fishermen who rented the fishings and destroyed their nets. The abbot had the provost and councillors summoned, on the authority of the Court of Session in Edinburgh, to appear before the abbot to explain themselves. Two years later the authority of the court was used to ensure that the abbey was recompensed.

Largely destroyed after the Reformation, little of the original abbey has survived in anything more than the floor plan, a gateway and the much restored late thirteenth- or early fourteenth-century bell tower – the only example of a free-standing belfry in Scotland. During the Reformation the abbey and its lands passed to Erskine, Earl of Mar, then Governor of Stirling Castle and Regent of Scotland. Some of the stonework was used in the extension of the castle and in the building of his house, Mar's Wark, in 1570.

from the parapets of Stirling Castle in 1507 in an attempt to impress him. Damian, known as 'The Leech', had already tried to turn lead into gold. Now he attempted to fly to France using wings made of feathers. When he plummeted from the battlements of Stirling Castle and broke his leg landing in a dungheap, he claimed that if he had used eagle feathers instead of hen feathers all would have been well.

It was said of James IV that he was 'more courageous than a king ought to be'. Allied with France, in 1513 James invaded England, which earned him excommunication by the Pope. His forces engaged the Earl of Sussex at Flodden Field, just south of the border, where James became the last British king to be killed in battle – along with 3 bishops, 11 earls, 15 lords and 10,000 men. His reign marked the end of the medieval period and the stage was set for modern history to begin. But in leaving an heir barely a year-and-a-half old, he had done his kingdom no great favour.

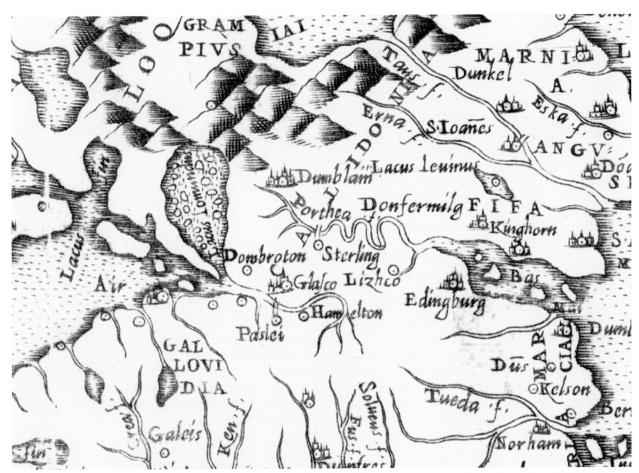

This is a portion of the oldest surviving printed map of Scotland shown on its own, dating from about 1570. It was probably engraved by Paolo Forlani of Venice and based on a 1546 outline map of the British Isles by George Lily, an English priest who had lived in Italy. The place names are probably taken from Hector Boece's *History of Scotland* with his imaginative spellings (Dunfermilg, Dombroton, etc.). The importance of Sterling (Stirling) Bridge is apparent from its prominent marking. The original map was given to the Royal Scottish Geographical Society in 1919 who sold it to the National Library of Scotland in 1992. Contrast this with Pont's map on p. 47. (*NLS*)

James V (born 1512, ruled 1513–42) began the Renaissance palace within the castle walls in 1540. (*SCLS*)

Clearly, all was not well in Stirling during the reign of James IV, at least from the point of view of one William Dunbar, who wrote this 'Dregy', or 'Dirge', in about 1490. A satirical rendition of the Mass for the Dead, it parodies 'Strivilling' (Stirling) as being like hell or purgatory on account of the small fish and poor wine, although admittedly it was composed by an Edinburgh man.

> Cum hame and dwell no moir in Strivilling
> From hiddeous hell cum hame and dwell
> Quhair fische to sell in non bot spirling
> Cum hame and dwell no moir in Strivilling
> Oh God, liberate thy children who live in
> The town of Stirling from its pains and sorrows,
> and bring them the joy of Edinburgh,
> That Stirling may be at rest.

James V and the Renaissance Palace

In 1540 James V (born 1512, ruled 1513–42) began the marvellous Renaissance palace and thereby turned Stirling Castle into one of the most sumptuous buildings in Scotland, commissioning French masons for much of the stonework. In the 1530s James also employed a French gardener at Stirling and the establishment of the King's Knot, the formal garden on the south façade, may date from then, although it is usually credited to his great-grandson, Charles I.

James V was just seventeen months old when he was crowned James V in Stirling Castle's chapel in 1513. James grew up literate, educated (at least up to the age of twelve) and cultured, but also spoilt and immoral, fathering at

THE KINGDOM OF KIPPEN

The picturesque parish and village of Kippen in the Fintry Hills some 10 miles west of Stirling is known locally as 'The Kingdom'. The name originated in the reign of James IV when the local laird, the childless Menzies of Arnprior, adopted John Buchanan as a baby to prevent the king acquiring his estate. The title 'The King of Kippen' was later bestowed upon Buchanan by James V. A story collected by Sir Walter Scott tells that the king sent his men to hunt venison from the nearby hills. On returning, they crossed land belonging to Buchanan, who had a number of guests with him, short of victuals but having taken of copious amounts of drink. Buchanan ambushed them and took the deer for his table. The hunters claimed that the venison belonged to the king, whereon Buchanan replied that James might be the King of Scotland but that he was the King of Kippen. James V was amused by this and

The famous Kippen Vine, planted in 1891 by local market gardener Duncan Buchanan, was said to be the largest in the world under glass and eventually covered about 5,000 square feet of roof space, producing 600 bunches of Gros Colman grapes by 1910 and 2,000 bunches by 1960. It stretched for 300 feet with a girth at its widest of 56 inches. It produced the best-quality table grapes but could not compete with cheaper imports. Duncan's son Selby broke up the vine in 1964 when the vineyard was sold. (*SCLS*)

rode to meet Buchanan, announcing that 'the Gudman of Ballengeich is come to feast with the King of Kippen'. They had a cordial time and Buchanan became a great favourite, often invited as 'King of Kippen' to meet his fellow sovereign at Stirling Castle. Buchanan remained a staunch ally of James and died in the service of his daughter Mary at the Battle of Pinkie in 1547. Later, Kippen was the scene of one of Rob Roy MacGregor's most daring cattle raids.

This 1900s postcard shows Buchanan Street, Kippen, named after John Buchanan, 'King of Kippen'. (*Stirling Council*)

least six or perhaps as many as ten illegitimate children and keeping bad company. His nobles thought him dissolute, vindictive and greedy, although the general populace seemed to like him. It was his habit to travel incognito, calling himself 'the Gudeman o' Ballengeich' (a reference to a steep pass at the back of Stirling Castle, where he was born) and he performed many legendary acts of charity.

The crushing defeat inflicted on the Scots by Henry VIII at Solway Moss in 1542 added to the distress James V already felt at the death of his infant sons the year before, the cannily named James and Arthur, and destroyed his spirit. He retired to Falkland Palace, where the news that his wife had borne him a girl provoked him to utter (according to legend): 'It cam wi' a lass and it will gang wi' a lass', a reference to the way the Scottish Crown had come into his family through Marjorie Bruce after the death of Margaret, Maid of Norway, and that no woman could ever rule the troubled kingdom. Scotland's last Catholic king died at Falkland, a broken man, a week after his daughter was born – the equally tragic Mary, Queen of Scots.

The Ladies Rock in the castle cemetery was the favourite spot from which the ladies of the palace could watch the royal tournaments held in the field below. A pyramid nearby commemorates those martyred in the cause of religious freedom. (*Stirling Council*)

Mary, Queen of Scots – Stirling's Queen

Queen Mary had a deep connection with Stirling. She was crowned there, lived in the castle for her first five years, visited many times and ensured that her son was brought up there and christened in the Chapel Royal.

It is likely that almost everything you have heard, read or seen in films about Mary is wrong, or at least a half-truth. She was a complex character who lived at a time when the political and religious situation became very difficult indeed. Born at Linlithgow Palace on 8 December 1542, Mary became queen when she was just a week old. She spent the first few years of her life, from 27 July 1543 to February 1548, safe in Stirling Castle, watched over by her guardian John Erskine, the Earl of Mar.

Mary was next in line to the English throne after Henry VIII's children. Seeing the inherent crisis in this, the Scottish nobles agreed that Mary should marry Henry VIII's son, the future Edward VI. But as soon as the treaty was settled in 1543, Catholics opposed to the match took the infant Mary to Stirling Castle, and, to Henry's rage, cancelled the arrangement. Mary was crowned Queen of Scots in Stirling's Old Chapel on 9 September 1543, when she was only nine months old.

In 1558 Mary married the Dauphin Francis and the next year he succeeded to the French throne, making Mary Queen of France as well as Scotland. But Francis made the tactical mistake of having himself declared

Opposite: Mary Stuart, Queen of Scots, born in 1542 and ruled until 1587. This rather idealised anonymous portrait of Mary was painted in Victorian times when she was revered as a romantic but tragic figure. Certainly, she was good-looking, tall, graceful and intelligent, and a great favourite at the French court. At this time, the spelling of the royal family name of Stewart changed to Stuart in keeping with the French influence Mary had introduced. (*BD*)

Darnley's House. This house at the bottom of Broad Street was owned by Erskine of Gogar and is said to be where Mary, Queen of Scots' second husband, Lord Darnley, lived when visiting. The royal party stayed at the castle. By the end of the 1500s it was owned by the Earl of Mar, hereditary Keeper of Stirling Castle. A century later Janet Kilbowie ran part of the house as a tavern and, as was typical in such buildings, a number of families shared the living accommodation. An unusual feature is the barrel-vaulted ground floor not connected to those above. It is currently a café. (*Stirling Council*)

John Cowane's house in St Mary's Wynd is often known as Queen Mary's Palace, although it was no such thing. More likely it was lodgings for foreign visitors and emissaries. Bought and extended by the Cowane family as their town house, John Cowane was born here in about 1570. At the time it must have enjoyed unrivalled views over the river to Abbey Craig and the Ochil Hills. Later the building housed a carpet factory and a school, but was unroofed in 1877 to save tax and never re-covered. (*SCLS*)

King of Scotland. In the event, Francis died of an ear infection in 1560, barely eighteen months after taking his throne.

Mary's first visit to Stirling Castle after her return to Scotland was on 13 September 1561. The next day her priests and clerks were assaulted in the Chapel Royal while the High Mass was being sung. Later that evening, Mary narrowly escaped death by fire or asphyxiation when she left a candle burning by her bedside, setting the curtains of her bed ablaze.

Despite the obvious religious tensions in Scotland, Mary's reign was successful and moderate at the beginning. However, in 1565 she was persuaded into another marriage to her second cousin Henry, Lord Darnley, a great-grandson of Henry VII but a Catholic. The spoiled, profligate, petulant and possibly homosexual Darnley became a puppet of Mary's enemies and was implicated in the stabbing to death of her Italian secretary, David Riccio (or Rizzio), in front of the heavily pregnant queen.

Even the birth of a son to Mary and Darnley (later to become James VI) did not improve their relationship, and Darnley withdrew from the court. Mary spent a lot of time in her childhood home, Stirling Castle. She had passed the summer of 1562, the autumn of 1563 and the spring of 1565 there, and in 1566 took her baby son to be lodged there in the care of her own former guardian, the Earl of Mar. James was christened on 17 December 1566, in a ceremony far more sumptuous than Mary's 'coronation' twenty-three years previously.

Earl Bothwell, presiding at the baptism, was a handsome, rugged Borders lord and fast becoming Mary's firm favourite. Soon after, Darnley was taken mysteriously ill and Mary moved him to lodgings in Kirk o' Field, just outwith the walls of Edinburgh. Apparently solicitous, she nursed him herself, although she was absent when, on 10 February 1567, Darnley was murdered by an explosion with gunpowder. Bothwell was widely considered to be the main instigator of Darnley's murder with Mary implicated. Three months later she was carried off by Bothwell to his Dunbar castle and they secretly married. This, alongside her waning popularity, led to her downfall.

Mary was held captive in England for almost twenty years. Finally, the English queen's hand was forced by talk of Catholic plots and Mary was beheaded at Fotheringhay Castle in Northamptonshire on 8 February 1587, at the age of forty-four. Despite the legends and various Hollywood retellings, Mary and Elizabeth never met.

James VI and I – Baptised in Stirling, Ruled in London

After Mary's son James was baptised in Stirling Castle in 1566 he spent much of his young life there in the care of the Earl of Mar, while rival factions fought for control of Scotland. James was less than a year old when he saw his mother for the last time, and thirteen months old when he was crowned King of Scotland after Mary's enforced abdication in his favour. The Protestant lords, led by the Earls of Mar, Morton and Home, wanted a quick coronation in a church that was safe, close to Stirling Castle, and non-Catholic. The answer was the Church of the Holy Rude. The coronation was held on 29 July 1567 with John Knox preaching a lengthy sermon on the slaying of Queen Ahaliah and the crowning of the young King Joab. The ceremony was carried out by the Bishop of Orkney in a record 20 minutes for fear of Catholic disruption, then the toddler king was returned to the safety of the castle.

Stirling Castle was attacked twice during the childhood of James VI – in 1571 and 1578. He was taken there, virtually a prisoner, after the Ruthven Raid of 1582, and the castle was besieged again in 1585. By this time, these

Mar's Wark. John Erskine, first Earl of Mar and Regent, started to build a Renaissance mansion close to the castle. Its size and position clearly indicate that it was intended to be a statement of his importance as one of the richest and most powerful men in Scotland and hereditary Governor of Stirling Castle. Mar died in 1572 and only the entrance and gate were ever completed. The main rooms were on the first floor and the frontage was richly decorated with sculptures and plasters, including a corpse wrapped in a shroud. The Earls of Mar lived in the building for the next century or so, after which it was used to house soldiers and in the 1730s the town council converted it into a workhouse (hence the derivation of Mar's Wark). Now only the façade stands. (BD)

REGENT MORTON AND STIRLING

Sir James Douglas, 4th Earl of Morton, was elected Regent in 1572. He was the second son of Sir George Douglas, younger brother of Archibald, 6th Earl of Angus. The marriage between the 6th Earl of Angus and Margaret of England, widow of James IV and sister of Henry VIII, brought the Douglas family into an alliance with England. During the reign of James V, most of them lived in exile, returning only after his death in 1542 and the accession of Mary, Queen of Scots. Morton himself was deeply involved in promoting re-formation and a marriage between Henry's son and the infant Mary. He inherited the Morton title from his father-in-law and was one of the most powerful nobles in Scotland, becoming Lord High Chancellor in 1563. He was an ally of Darnley in the murder of David Riccio and of the regents Moray and Lennox, events that destabilised Scotland again. Lennox was assassinated in 1572 during an audacious night raid on a king's party parliament at Stirling, to be succeeded by the far more conciliatory Mar. In 1571 Douglas fought off the storming of Stirling by Queen Mary's party, and might have become Regent at that point (he was Queen Elizabeth's choice) but the title went to Stirling's Governor, Erskine of Mar. However, Morton became Regent the next year. Brutally effective during the minority of James VI, his fortune turned when he was accused of complicity in the murder of Darnley, the king's father, although his real crime may have been to debase the Scots currency by manipulating the proportion of sterling silver. Or it may have been the fourteen-year-old King James exerting his authority. Morton was executed in 1581 by an instrument called the maiden, which he himself had introduced into Scotland. His head was displayed at the public gaol, and his body was taken to the burial ground for criminals.

depredations, combined with a general lack of maintenance, had led to some of the buildings deteriorating into a state of near-collapse. The Chapel Royal was in poor condition and also sat at an unusual angle. Using a Musselburgh architect, the appropriately named William Wallace, who worked on many royal projects, James built a new chapel, completed in time for the baptism of Henry, his first son by Anne of Denmark, in 1594. But when he succeeded to the English throne in 1603 at the Union of the Crowns Stirling Castle's role as a royal residence was effectively ended. James moved his court to Whitehall Palace in London and the area around it became known as 'Scotland Yard'. James had promised to return often to Scotland, but in fact did so only once, in 1617. However, this caused significant work to be carried out at the castle to make it suitable for his visit.

James VI's fear of witchcraft is well known. He wrote various books and tracts on the subject and persecuted 'witches'. One of the victims of this was Alison Pearson of Byrehill, whose trial record bears a note in the margin: '*Convicta et combusta*' (convicted and burned). Pearson was tried on 28 May 1588 for invocation of the spirits of the devil, specially the vision of her cousin William Sympson, said to be a great scholar and doctor of medicine, dispensing charms and remedies but rooking the ignorant. Pearson's own confession was the principal evidence in this time of superstition and anti-Catholic hysteria.

Pearson's familiar in the court of Elfland, William Sympson, was born in Stirling where his father was the king's smith. It was said that William had been taken as a child by a 'man of Egypt' (Gipsy), who kept him for twelve years, and that his father died in the meantime for 'opening a priest's book and looking upon it'. Pearson confessed that she had renewed her acquaintance with her kinsman as soon as he returned. One day as she was

Pont's 1590 map of 'Starling and Starling Castel' features recognisable buildings, including the Church of the Holy Rude. Timothy Pont was born in the mid-sixteenth century (possibly in 1564), son of the Reverend Robert Pont of Shiresmill, Fife, an eminent minister, lawyer and writer. In 1580 Timothy first attended St Andrews University and learned the art of map making and began travelling and mapping following his graduation. These were the first detailed maps of Scotland and were the basis of the first atlas of Scotland produced by Joan Blaeu as part of his world atlas, *Theatrum orbis terrarum, sive Atlas novus*. On Pont's death (possibly in 1614) the maps were acquired by his heirs and by 1629 they were sold to the Lord Lyon King-of-Arms, historian Sir James Balfour. The noted scholar and statesman Sir John Scot of Scotstarvit knew that the Amsterdam map maker Joan Blaeu was looking for maps of Scotland and put him in touch with Balfour. Blaeu used thirty-six of them. After the maps were returned to Scotland they passed, via the Gordon family and Scotland's Geographer Royal, Sir Robert Sibbald, to the Advocates Library in Edinburgh and in 1925 to the Scottish nation for the newly established National Library of Scotland, which has seventy-seven individual maps on thirty-eight sheets. (*NLS*)

walking through Grange Muir she had a fit and lay down. A green man appeared to her, and said he would help her if she would be faithful to him. He disappeared but soon returned to her with many other men and women who took the bemused and frightened Alison, against her will she claimed, further than she could tell, as far as Lothian. She saw piping, dancing, mirth, the taking of wine with tassies (drinking cups) but when she later told this to others she suffered a stroke that affected her left side and left an ugly mark with no feeling. She also confessed that she had seen the 'good neighbours' make magic salves before sunrise with pans and fires. Sometimes they came to her in fearful forms and threatened to murder her if she told of them, but at other times they spoke well to her and promised her rewards if she remained faithful. Pearson boasted of her favour with the Queen of Elfland and her good friends at the Faerie Court. She said that William Sympson told her when the Fair Folk were coming and taught her about remedies and their application. Patrick Adamson, created Archbishop of St Andrews by James VI, took her nostrums – eating a stewed fowl and drinking medicated claret, which, according to the belief of the time, transferred the cleric's illness to a white palfrey which then died. Adamson was charged with behaviour unbecoming to his order. Pearson also claimed to have seen Lethington and Buccleuch in Elfland. If the latter was a reference to 'Wicked Wat' (Walter Scott of Buccleuch), it may have been justified. But if it was implicating his great-grandson, 'Bold Buccleuch', created Lord Scott of Buccleuch by James VI, she picked a bad time to mis-call one of the king's favourites.

Charles I and the Covenanters

King James VI and I was succeeded by Charles I in 1625 and more work was carried out in expectation of a royal visit. After all, he had been born in Dunfermline and would naturally want to see his native land. This was not to happen until June 1633 and only on one further occasion in 1641. Had Charles spent more time in Scotland and understood why the Calvinist Church had no desire to be close to English bishops, he might not have found himself opposed by Covenanters. By 1645 his affairs in England were also much in decline, with Parliament harrying him. The Earl of Montrose fought for Charles in Scotland (he was immediately created Marquis of Montrose and appointed commander-in-chief) and formed an army with several of the northern clans. Marching south, Montrose passed by Stirling, not just because the castle was occupied by the Covenanters, but because the plague was raging in the town. He later engaged the enemy at Kilsyth, some 12 miles south-west of Stirling. The Covenanter force was 6,000 foot and 1,000 horse strong, whereas Montrose had not much more than half those numbers. But he had the advantage of the ground and also of tactics – Montrose ordered his men to strip to their shirts, tied between their legs, so that their broadswords would be unencumbered and they could run faster in pursuit of the enemy. This gave rise to the tradition, still current, that the army of Montrose fought naked. The battle was a total rout and few of the Covenanter infantry escaped death or capture while Montrose lost only seven

or eight of his men. But it scarcely mattered because Charles surrendered to the Scots in 1646, expecting more sympathetic treatment, but was handed over to the English. By 1649 he had been executed by Parliament.

Argyll's Lodging, which dates from this period, is one of the most important seventeenth-century town houses surviving in Scotland. At the time when Stirling was still a royal court many of the nobles who had estates nearby also built or rented 'ludgins' (town houses) near the castle to be close to the king. The building known as Argyll's Lodging may date from the early 1600s but was bought and extended by the Earl of Stirling in about 1632. Before this he had been Sir William Alexander of Menstrie, Governor of Nova Scotia and later created 1st Earl of Stirling and Viscount Canada. He also held the post of Secretary of State for Scotland. The carved stone panel above the main entrance bears the Earl of Stirling's coat of arms combined with the flag of Nova Scotia on a shield supported by a Native American brave.

The Earl of Stirling had travelled widely with the Earl of Argyll, who acquired the house in the 1650s. Arygll extended it further, mostly on the western and southern sides, and enclosed the courtyard. His boar's head crest can be seen above the windows. Despite these and later alterations, the house retains many of the typical features of the period – dormer windows, crow-stepped gables, round towers with turnpike stairs and intricate stone carving on the door and window frames.

The house saw many famous and infamous visitors. Charles II stayed here before his coronation at Scone in 1651, the second Duke of Argyll set up his headquarters in the building in 1715 before the Battle of Sheriffmuir and

Argyll's Lodging. The picture postcard shows Argyll's Lodging during the Second World War when it was used as a military hospital. The Duke of York (later James VII) stayed here in 1680 with his daughter Queen Anne, who oversaw the Union of Parliaments in 1704. James repaid Argyll's hospitality by having him beheaded in 1685. (BD)

HOLY RUDE

The Church of the Holy Rude (Holy Cross) is the oldest building in Stirling after the castle and is probably the only church in Britain apart from Westminster Abbey to have hosted a coronation and still be in use today. It dates back to the reign of David I (1124–53), although the present building was begun after the great fire of 1405, which virtually destroyed Stirling. The first stage, including the nave and tower, was completed in about 1470 and the remainder by 1555. As the parish church of Stirling and with close links with the castle, it benefited from the support and patronage of the Stuart kings. On 29 July 1567 James VI and I was crowned here as an infant, to ensure his succession after his mother Mary, Queen of Scots. It was felt important by the Protestant nobles then in the ascendant to have him crowned in a Reformed church, especially since his baptism had been according to Catholic rites in the castle's Chapel Royal. John Knox preached here regularly (and, it is said, interminably). On 24 May 1997 Queen Elizabeth attended a re-enactment of the coronation of 430 years before and unveiled a commemorative plaque to mark the event.

Kings and queens have always worshipped there alongside the townspeople. At one time 2,000 people could be accommodated in 2 separate congregations, by ingenious use of galleries and a dividing wall. This was much needed in medieval times, when church services went on almost continuously – apart from regular services there were private masses, special services for trade guilds, corporations and other bodies – and when there were disputes between factions in the congregation. The partition was taken away during renovations in 1936. Now opened out internally, Holy Rude looks and feels more like a cathedral, with magnificent stained-glass windows and one of Scotland's few surviving medieval open timber roofs.

Holy Rude also fulfilled the other typical roles of a church of its day – providing education, relief for the poor, help for the sick, sanctuary for the refugee and outlaw and chapel to the guilds and trades. Each guild would have maintained an altar to its patron saint and wealthy burgesses built their own chapels. The vaulted Chapel of St Andrew survives intact. The organ – the largest in Scotland – has 4,297 pipes, 4 manuals and pedals, 82 speaking stops and 24 couplers. Built in Liverpool by Rushworth and Dreaper in 1939, it was completely refurbished by the same firm in 1994. It is used regularly for services and also for recitals.

The Church of the Holy Rude – Stirling's 'cathedral'. (*BD*)

'Butcher' Cumberland stayed there on his way to massacre the Scots at Culloden in 1746. Now, the rooms are furnished as they would have been during the 9th Earl of Argyll's time (in about 1680).

Restoration and Rebellion

In 1651, two years after his father's execution, Charles II was declared King of Scotland and crowned at Scone, some 35 miles from Stirling. Oliver Cromwell had already sent an army north in 1650. Stirling Castle was besieged and taken by General Monk the following year, during which time the fabric of the castle sustained a great deal of damage. Monk made Stirling his base for the collection of the Register of the Scottish Kingdom to send to London. A local tall tale, recounted by Mr Finlayson, town clerk towards the end of the seventeenth century, tells that when Cromwell's army was at Airth a cannon fired a ball at Stirling which stuck in the bell of a trumpet sounded by one of the castle soldiers. Far from being injured, the trumpeter blew a loud note and sent the ball back, killing the artilleryman who had fired it. Charles II never visited Scotland after his restoration in 1660, but sent his brother, James, Duke of York and Albany (later King James VII and II). He visited Stirling in February 1681 but the castle was too dilapidated for him to stay there.

In 1685 the Duke of York succeeded his brother as King James VII and II, but fled three years later when his daughter Mary Stewart and her husband, William of Orange, arrived to take over the throne jointly. This put an end to more than three centuries of Stewart rule in Scotland, but it was the start of a new conflict. Rebellion broke out almost immediately by the predominantly Catholic Jacobites under the leadership of John Graham of Claverhouse, Viscount Dundee. His campaign ended with a victory at the Battle of Killiecrankie in 1689, although Claverhouse himself died. But the uprising had highlighted certain weaknesses in several Scottish castles, including Stirling and improvements were put in hand to take account of modern warfare – artillery positions were installed on the eastern side and two lesser entrances were closed off.

On the death of James VII (James II of Britain) in 1701 his son, James VIII, known as the Old Pretender, carried on the Stewart family's claim to the thrones of Scotland and England. The Act of Union in 1707, under Queen Anne (the first monarch of Great Britain and Ireland), caused great resentment in Scotland – it effectively ended Scotland's separate political identity – and James seized the opportunity this presented him to gather support. A fleet of ships and soldiers provided by Louis XIV of France (who saw his chance to harry England) sailed up the Forth on 23 March 1708. The expected local support failed to materialise but the threat led to more fortification and defensive improvement in Scottish castles. Between 1708 and 1714, the east side of Stirling Castle was strengthened, building on the outer defences erected in the 1550s for Mary of Guise. The castle's then governor, John, 6th Earl of Mar, submitted plans for royal lodgings and accommodation for himself, but these were rejected by the Hanoverian rulers. This clearly irked Mar, who raised the standard of the Old Pretender at Braemar on 6 September 1715 and

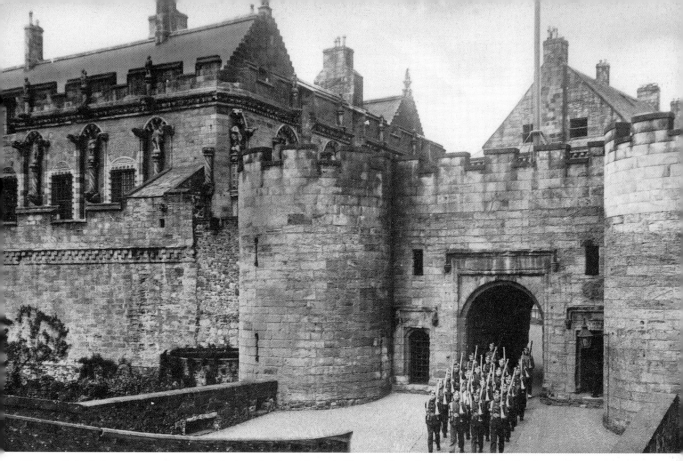

The castle's defences were improved during the Jacobite rebellions. After the restoration of Charles II the castle had reverted to the Earl of Mar and his heirs as hereditary Keepers, but the Earl was accused of being a Jacobite and King George I removed him from his charge. The Crown became the Keeper. When Queen Victoria visited Stirling in 1849 she described the castle as 'extremely grand'. The castle's architectural subtleties came to be appreciated more and more and in 1906 King Edward VII suggested that its maintenance should be transferred from the War Office to the Office of Works. In 1923, King George V restored the Earl of Mar as Keeper once again. Now it is in the care of Historic Scotland. (*SCLS*)

sparked off the second Jacobite rising. Mar was defeated at Sheriffmuir, a battle he would have won if he had had any military skill whatsoever. The Duke of Argyll had raised an army of 1,500 in the King's Park and marched them over Stirling Bridge and a few miles north to defeat Mar.

The improved defences were next tested during the third Jacobite rising in 1745. James's son Charles Edward Stuart arrived to continue his father's cause and his army exchanged fire with Stirling Castle's defenders as it marched south. Charles and his nobles stayed at Bannockburn House, by invitation of Sir Hugh Paterson, nephew of the Earl of Mar, which accounted for his attachment to the Stewart cause.

The Jacobite army took Edinburgh, won a victory at Preston, reached as far south into the heart of England as Derby and looked for a while as though they might prevail. But they were forced to return north and in January 1746 Charles made Bannockburn House his headquarters, with his troops billeted in neighbouring villages. Lord George Murray occupied Falkirk. The Stirling magistrates surrendered but the Revd Ebenezer Erskine commanded two companies of the townsmen, armed and supported by the castle's defenders. French cannon had arrived at Montrose, were shipped to Perth and

Opposite: The Clan MacRae memorial at Sheriffmuir, erected in memory of those MacRaes who died defending 'The Royal House of Stuart' in 1715. (*Stirling Council*)

The Argyll Highlanders memorial at Stirling Castle. (*BD*)

were brought across the Forth, partly at the ford of Frew, and partly at Alloa. The prince started a tedious but necessary siege against Stirling Castle. Eventually the town was taken – with the burghers winning concessions that they would not be punished, molested or robbed – but the castle held out against the Jacobite rebels.

Despite winning an infantry victory at what came to be known as the Second Battle of Falkirk in January 1746 against Lieutenant-General Hawley (although it was little more than an undignified skirmish, at least from the Hanoverian perspective), the Jacobites were eventually pursued north to Culloden by the Duke of Cumberland, a prince of the blood. Marching from Linlithgow, he heard two explosions from the direction of Stirling. It was Charles's powder magazines. The Jacobites were forced to spike their heavy cannon and abandon the siege of Stirling Castle. Although they had captured the town, the castle had resisted them, and knowing a larger English force was on the way, the Jacobite army left. An arch of the Stirling Old Bridge had been broken by the governor, General Blackney (or Blakeney), in December 1745 to prevent Charles's northern armies from crossing and the rebels had not found a decent place to site the batteries of cannon. Once again, Stirling Castle had proved all but impregnable. Blackney was, in fact, almost at the end of his supplies and ammunition and could not have held out much longer. But Charles Stuart did not know that.

Brigadier Mordaunt took possession of Stirling and next day the Duke of Cumberland ordered the bridge to be repaired. On 4 February, he marched his army north and routed the Highlanders in the massacre of Culloden, which lasted no more than 25 minutes and ended almost fifty years of Stewart attempts to regain the throne of Scotland. Prince Charles Edward Lewis Philip Cassimir Mary-Silvester Stuart died, a despondent drunk, in Rome on 31 January 1788, at the age of sixty-seven.

The Argyll Highlanders

Stirling Castle never again served as a defence against siege, but it assumed another important role at the end of the eighteenth century. In 1794 war in France broke out and Campbell of Lochnell mustered the Duke of Argyll's Highland Regiment in Stirling Castle. Barracks accommodation was provided by inserting additional floors and walls in the Great Hall and the original roof was replaced. The Chapel Royal became storage space. New buildings were added, including the Fort Major's House, the Guardhouse, a Master Gunner's House in the Outer Close and powder magazines in the nether bailey. It ceased to be a military post in 1964 but the King's Old Building still houses the Argyll and Sutherland Highlanders' regimental headquarters and museum. An extensive programme of repair and restoration started in the 1960s and upkeep continues under the aegis of Historic Scotland.

4

The Shaping of Stirling Burgh

Stirling's shape and structure reflects its changing role over the centuries. As a defensive fort, the town was synonymous with the castle on the rock. During the 700 years up to the Stewarts, Stirling had had many of the characteristics of a frontier town in the Wild West. Mainly built of wood, it was often burned – we know about devastating fires in 1244, 1298, 1385 and 1406. With the coming of the royal residence, there was an upsurge in stonework to house the courtiers and the many tradesmen and craft workers needed to support them. These were necessarily clustered around and near the castle, within the ports and gates built into defensive walls below the castle itself. The town wall was erected as a defence against English invasions in 1457. Stirling and the surrounding area became the site of many feudal castles and religious houses and a number of the nobles and estate owners also built town houses near the castle. The 'Top of the Town' near the castle was the centre of commercial, public and social life. Although many of the buildings that housed the less wealthy have been swept away in the ensuing centuries, a number of the 'ludgins' (lodgings, or town houses) of wealthy nobles and merchants survive, as well as other public and civic buildings. Stirling's parish church, the Church of the Holy Rude, dates from the 1450s and nestles close to the castle.

Among the lords and burgesses who built, bought or rented properties nearby were: the Earl of Mar, hereditary Keeper of Stirling Castle, who started Mar's Wark in 1569 but never completed it; Robert Bruce of Auchenbowie, Provost of Stirling in the 1550s; and the Earl of Stirling, who built and later sold the house known as Argyll's Lodging to the Earl of Argyll. The seventeenth-century Darnley's House was where Lord Darnley is said to have stayed when visiting Mary, Queen of Scots.

After the departure of the royal court in 1603 the various businesses looked beyond the castle for trade but continued to live within its defensive walls and ditches. The earliest town plans, Pont's map of 1590 and Laye's 1725 plan, show a structure essentially unchanged with only a few buildings outwith the Barras Yett (Burgh Gate) at what is now the junction of Dumbarton Road and Port Street. John Cowane's House (also known as Queen Mary's Palace) and

The unicorn figure on top of the Mercat Cross is known locally as the 'puggy' for a reason no one now remembers. Neither the puggy nor its name are unique to Stirling – Prestonpans, for instance, has a column like the Stirling one with a similarly named unicorn. Puggy is an old Scots word for a monkey or sometimes a kitten, but this fails to explain its usage in this context. (*Stirling Council*)

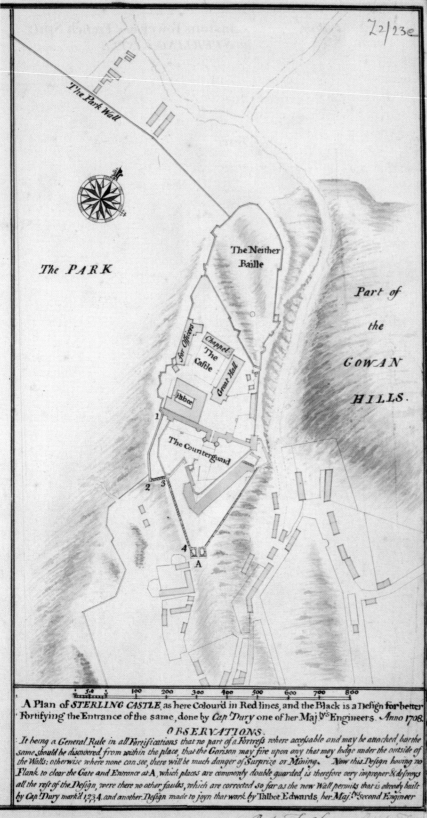

Anti-Union feelings post-1707 and the abortive Stuart uprising in 1708 led to an upgrading of the defences of important Scottish castles, notably Stirling, Edinburgh and Fort William, by Captain Theodore Dury, who produced plans of the fortifications. The Board of Ordnance also had drawn up detailed road maps and town plans which were useful during the later Jacobite rebellions. A section of the 'Plan of the Town and Castle of Sterling' in 1725 is seen here. (*NLS*)

John Cowane's Hospital and the house of Robert Spittal, James VI's tailor, and Norie's House all date from the mid-seventeenth century.

At the foot of Broad Street the Mercat Cross was the site of the weekly market, the annual fair and the place of public execution, handy for the Tolbooth gaol. The Mercat Cross was also where royal proclamations were read and where the town councillors used the excuse of royal birthdays and other anniversaries to drink numerous toasts. It was also where criminals were put in the stocks, pilloried or executed. The last public execution in 1843 caused outrage when 83-year-old Allan Mair, despite his infirmities, almost managed to struggle free of the rope and had to be dispatched by the hangman pulling on his legs. The market here, founded in 1226, was where farmers sold produce like oats, fruits and eggs. Meat and fish were sold at the fleshmercat.

As the burgh's main gathering place, the Mercat Cross was also the site of riots and demonstrations, including those against the Union of Parliaments in

NORIE'S HOUSE

Norie's House dates from the time when Stirling was starting to expand beyond its defensive walls and think about trade, but important burgesses still wanted to be in a central position. James Norie was the town clerk and a lawyer, as can be seen from the bewigged stone head peering down from near the top of the roof, as if he were keeping a posthumous eye on the goings on of the burgh and the Tolbooth across Broad Street. On the frontage are initials including those of Norie and his wife and mottos such as 'Arbor vitae sapientia' – 'Wisdom is the tree of life'.

This tall house was built in 1671 on land belonging to Norie's wife's family and is typical of the period although having its own well made it extremely modern and fashionable. It was also in the right spot for civic entertainment – royal proclamations would have been read at the Mercat Cross just outside, where criminals were put in the stocks, pilloried or even publicly executed. Broad Street was a bustling hive of activity at the time. Outside and to the front of these buildings there would have been wooden booths – the late-medieval equivalent of shops. Narrow pends (roofed closes) led to the back yards and thin plots of land used as kitchen gardens, where the occupants kept hens and other livestock and grew vegetables. Most of the neighbouring houses have been demolished or rebuilt. Over the years these were knocked together and several families would have shared a building.

Norie's House. (*Stirling Council*)

Broad Street and the Mercat Cross. (*SCLS*)

1707 and during the hangings of the Radical Rebellion. The street was a hive of activity and trade and therefore filled with refuse. Open gutters down each side of the road carried sewage to the river and were a haven for vermin and disease which then infested the crowded dwellings all around. In dry weather rubbish had to be taken away by horse cart.

Trade and the Tolbooth

When the burgh walls ceased to have a defensive function, they became the means to regulate trade in and out of the burgh. The town was spreading beyond the sixteenth-century walls and something akin to its present structure started to emerge. As with most Scottish towns, the Tolbooth also served as a prison, armoury, burgh treasury and council chambers. In 1689 the existing two-storey Tolbooth was declared by the town council to be 'ruinous' (presumably meaning in a ruined state rather than expensive to maintain) and was torn down in about 1700. At about the same time a new bell had been ordered from Holland for the town clock in the steeple and Duncan Kerr of Falkirk was commissioned to make a new clock and a year later to provide a new staff, globe and weathercock.

The current Tolbooth was built between 1703 and 1705 and combined its function as a customs house with those of burgh council chambers, courthouse and town gaol. It was designed in the then-popular 'classical manner' by Sir William Bruce, who was also the architect of Holyrood Palace. The Dutch pavilion roof is one of the oldest surviving in Scotland. Built facing onto Broad Street, it was extended eastwards with three bays by architect Gideon Gray in 1785 and again between 1806 and 1811 by Edinburgh architect Richard Crichton, with a courthouse and gaol added to the south fronting onto Gaol Wynd and St John Street. Prisoners sentenced

Stirling's Tolbooth, seen from an unusual perspective. (*Stirling Council*)

to die were hung at the Mercat Cross outside and some are said to be buried under the foundations. Not surprisingly, the Tolbooth is reputed to be haunted by the ghosts of the interred, and many visitors have heard footsteps and felt a sudden icy cold. Despite the fine stone fireplace in one of the first-floor rooms and a landscape painted in oils directly onto the panelling above it, the conditions in the new prison were condemned as the worst in Scotland by government inspectors. In 1864 the burgh council ordered a recast of the 1698 16-foot belfry bell and in addition a chime of

This montage shows some of the doctors who worked at the Stirling Royal Infirmary in the late nineteenth century, including the redoubtable Dr William Hutton Forrest who forced the adoption of clean water and decent sewerage in the town. He was presented with a silver tea service in 1857 for his efforts. (*BD*)

sixteen bells. The council continued to hold its meetings in the Tolbooth until 1875 by which time the prison had been moved to the Old Town Gaol in St John Street. Recently, thanks to a lottery grant, the Tolbooth has been renovated as a base for Stirling Council's Heritage & Cultural Services and become the main venue in Stirling for performing arts, cinema and other cultural activities. The internal courtyard was enclosed, creating a 200-seat auditorium with meeting rooms, recording studio, rehearsal space, bar and restaurant. During the renovations in 2001 a hidden staircase was found in the courtroom (now the main auditorium) which may have been the stair up which prisoners were led into the court to hear their sentences. Alternatively, its main purpose may have been to allow the jury members to go directly to the courtroom above. The historic stairwell is now behind a glass viewing panel in the reception area.

Alexander Bowie

During the late eighteenth and early nineteenth centuries, Stirling's industries – mostly based on water, such as weaving, tanning and brewing – developed strong links and trade routes via the River Forth with Holland and Scandinavia. Elegant Georgian suburbs emerged and turnpikes replaced the old cart tracks and drove roads into the town. The 1788 Old Grammar School dates from this period and is indicative of the growth of the population and its need for improved amenities.

One of the unsung heroes of Stirling's development is Alexander Bowie, builder and architect. Born in Muthill, Perthshire, Bowie moved to Stirling in 1803 and, in order to work within the burgh, applied in 1804 to join the Incorporation of Mechanics, the trades society for masons, slaters, plasterers, carvers, coopers, dyers and other 'wrights'. During the next few years following his becoming a burgess, Bowie worked mainly on jobbing contracts as well as repairs and alterations to existing buildings. He was involved in the building of the New Town Gaol and extensions to the Tolbooth. Bowie made an astute marriage to Margaret Hill, daughter of Alexander Hill, a well-known local maltster, burgess and guild brother and niece of Robert Gillies, twice Provost of Stirling (1823 and 1824) and therefore well connected in a way that Bowie himself was not. But while it might be assumed that they were genuinely fond of each other as Margaret bore ten children between 1808 and 1825, the strain seems to have killed her as she died of consumption in 1826 aged only forty.

In 1814 Bowie drew up plans for a mealmarket which were never used – Allan Johnston's Athenaeum (also called The Steeple) at the head of King Street was constructed instead. However, Bowie's most significant building work began with the planned development of Allan Park.

In 1816 the council decided to culvert the town burn where it flowed through Allan Park from the King's Park to the Forth, along Dumbarton Road to the Burgh Gate and under the line of the town wall. Bowie acquired a plot on the east corner of Allan Park and Dumbarton Road and built 1–9 Allan Park and 35 and 37 Dumbarton Road, naming the block Wellington Place, Allan Park. The building instructions laid down by the feu superiors (a trust for the relief of poor boys) required the houses to be 20 feet high on two floors with regular hewn doors and windows and slate roofs. In the event, and inspired by Edinburgh's New Town, Bowie constructed distinctive houses with ashlar sandstone – rather than the local brown whinstone from the castle rock quarries – with a common façade, classical pillars and pediments, rusticated stonework, detailed carving, segmental arched features, fanlights and railings typical of the Georgian town house. These and the block containing numbers 2, 4 and 6, built in about 1826, are Stirling's only examples of Georgian terraced houses. Historic Scotland listed them as being of architectural importance in 1965. By the time of his death in 1829, Bowie had erected fourteen of Allan Park's twenty-two houses. But his influence was profound – other distinctive sandstone Georgian houses reflecting the 'Allan Park style' were built in Upper Bridge Street and Melville Terrace, but not necessarily by Bowie.

The sandstone, which lent itself well to ornate carving, is best seen in Craigs House, built in about 1817 for Bowie's wife's uncle, Robert Gillies, owner of the tannery opposite. It was later a Masonic hall, the night club Le Clique during the 1970s and subsequently a Fat Sam's restaurant. Its dignity has been restored as the Bank of Scotland's Stirling branch. Bowie used stone from his own sandstone quarry at Thorndyke and his flagstone quarry at Drumhead, both near Denny, a half-dozen miles from Stirling. To work the stones, Bowie established a stoneyard behind his Allan Park site between Port Street and Dumbarton Road.

In 1827 Bowie constructed the neo-classical Commercial Bank located at 39 Spittal Street, to a design of William Stirling of Dunblane. It was his most prestigious public building work. In 1874 it became the first royal infirmary of Stirling, was later the education department offices and is currently the headquarters of Forth Valley Health Board. During the excavations for the foundations workmen unearthed Roman remains. The real spur to the development of a hospital for Stirling was the outbreak of disease in the 1830s.

Population Growth

An unusually high proportion of Stirling's population – about 8 per cent – was on some form of poor relief. Thanks to foundations like those of Spittal and Cowane and, later, bequests by John Allan in the 1720s and Alexander Cunningham in 1809, the funds available were large. The abolition of thirlage (effectively serfdom) in 1799 meant that vagrants could no longer be pressed into service. Economic migrants from the Highlands and returning soldiers swelled into the burgh. The castle was a hospital for wounded army veterans, some of whom had pensions. Anyone qualifying as a resident (three years) and as 'regularly' poor could receive a substantial income, greater, for example, than the daily female wage. This early version of the 'benefit trap' contributed to unemployment and, as ever, unemployment contributed to squalor, alcoholism and disease. The poor clustered in slum conditions around the castle rock just as the middle classes were starting to expand the lower town. Together, the well-off and worse-off combined to swell the population from under 4,000 in 1750 to over 12,000 a century later. Unemployment, the outlawing of trades unions (a measure instituted as a war-time measure but continued after 1815) and the passing of the Corn Laws, which kept prices high for the benefit of landowners, inevitably led to social foment and culminated in the Radical Rebellions in which Stirling played a crucial and bloody part.

As the town grew, there was increasing pressure on public services of all kinds, which came to a head in the 1830s. Squalid living conditions contributed to epidemics of influenza and cholera. The blame was placed on the water from St Ninian's Well and from the Butt Well behind the castle and measures were put in hand to improve the water supply. This resulted in the opening of a new reservoir at Touch and later, in the 1850s, to a general underground sewerage system, largely thanks to the efforts of Dr W.H. Forrest who drove the programme on despite cavilling, jealousy and outright prejudice from all corners. Poor relief was outstripping the burgh's ability to

THE ARMS OF STIRLING

The symbolism of the gate tower on the grassy mound are an obvious reference to the castle on the rock. The tree branches represent the Forest of Stirling, presumably part of the ancient Caledonian forest, although its precise site and boundaries are unknown. Traces of it can still be seen around – for instance at Murray's Wood in the Castle Park and near Bannockburn. The motto comes from the last two lines of a poem dating from 1296 or earlier.

Anglos a Scotis separat crux ista remotis
Hie armis Bruti: Scoti stant hic cruce tuti
Continet hoc in se nemus
Et castrum Strivilense.

The Britons stand by force of arms
The Scots are by this cross preserved from harm
The castle and Bridge of Stirling town
Are in the compass of this seal set down.

However, the first two lines are said to date originally from the invasion by Osbrecht and Ella, two Northumbrian princes, along with the Cumbrian Britons and Picts exiled in England, in the aftermath of the death of Kenneth MacAlpin in 855. They took Jedburgh but Kenneth's brother Donald, now king, defeated them and occupied Berwick where he complacently thought he would be safe. The Northumbrians surprised his army and took the king prisoner. They encountered little further resistance on their march north to Stirling where the Scots obtained a peace treaty on condition of paying a large sum of money (literally a king's ransom) and surrendering their possessions south of the Forth to Northumbria, and south of the Clyde plus Dumbarton to the Cumbrians. Osbrecht and Ella rebuilt Stirling Castle and a stone bridge over the Forth on which they raised a cross bearing the first two lines of the above inscription. Osbrecht and Ella both died in 866 while attacking York, then occupied by Danish Vikings.

The arms of Stirling. (*BD*)

support it. All of this, and the passing of the Police Acts in 1833, made it necessary to charge rates to pay for these new services. Fortunately, the new and reforming 'Tory' government of George IV had liberalised trade and employment conditions and now a burgh like Stirling was in a position to collect its own local taxes.

Any resentment among the public at having their purses felt was softened in 1837 when King William IV was succeeded by the eighteen-year-old Victoria. There was a new mood of entrepreneurship, a can-do mentality and, for the first time in almost a hundred years, hope for the future. Stirling Council even managed to find £20 to pay for a celebratory dinner, which it then ate, despite a complaint of squandering from the Stirling Working Men's Association. However, when Victoria visited Stirling five years later the poor were treated to a feast of roasted ox and beer on the Bowling Green at the Guildhall.

The pressure on building was such that the burgh spread outwards and its boundaries touched, and then absorbed, villages such as St Ninians, Causewayhead, Bridge of Allan and Torbrex, once very separate communities, and made them part of the bigger Stirling. As the county town and main market centre for the area, there was a need for Stirling to build new shops and business premises. It was during the Victorian era that most of Britain changed at a greater pace than ever before and Stirling was no exception. It is worth remembering that when Queen Victoria came to the throne she had available to her more or less the same communications technologies as Julius Caesar. Yet by the end of her reign she was travelling through Stirling by rail and improved roads. When Her Majesty visited Stirling Castle in 1849 she pronounced it to be 'extremely grand'. The queen's affection for nearby Braemar and Royal Deeside gave the already burgeoning tourist industry a welcome boost and a fashionable spin.

Stirling's Schools

It says something about Stirling's egalitarian outlook and its belief in education that in 2002 both its Westminster MP and its MSP were female and both they and the First Minister of the Scottish Parliament (previously leader of Stirling Council) were ex-teachers. A school has existed in Stirling since at least the twelfth century when the Bishop of St Andrews, in whose diocese Stirling sat, gave the churches of Perth and Stirling and their schools to Queen Margaret's Church of the Holy Trinity in Dunfermline (now Dunfermline Abbey). Later charters mention a 'scholam de Striuelin' but where this Church school stood is unknown as almost all the old town's buildings, except the castle, were destroyed by fire in 1405. In about 1450 the burgh built a thatched single-storey school on the south side of the Castle Hill, which would be the site of the establishment until 1856. Education was limited in scope, open to few and expensive, but there were various sources of financial aid to make schooling available to children from poor families.

A grammar school, or its predecessor, is first mentioned in the burgh records of 1523. Until the Reformation of 1560, the Abbot of Dunfermline appointed the Magister (master), but the town council administered it. The

The Old Grammar School on the Castle Hill site, now The Portcullis. (*NP*)

This photograph and those on p. 68 show the High School, which is actually four different buildings. The Academy Road frontage (seen here) dates from 1854, the Elementary School and Spittal Street wing from 1887–9 and the Primary School at the Back Walk end of Academy Road from 1907. In the 1850s ex-pupil Colonel Tovey Tennant offered £1,000 to the council for improvements to the site, which then contained the Writing School, the Trades Hall (1750) and the place where livestock was butchered, the blood and waste running downhill in an open channel. The original designs by Hay of Liverpool were for a quadrangle, but lack of funds meant that the Spittal Street building and its observatory were not erected for thirty years, designed by another ex-pupil, James Marjoribanks MacLaren, who died aged thirty-seven before seeing it finished.

The High School, now
the Stirling Highland
Hotel, with its
observatory donated by
Henry Campbell
Bannerman, local MP
and later Prime Minister.
(*Stirling Council*)

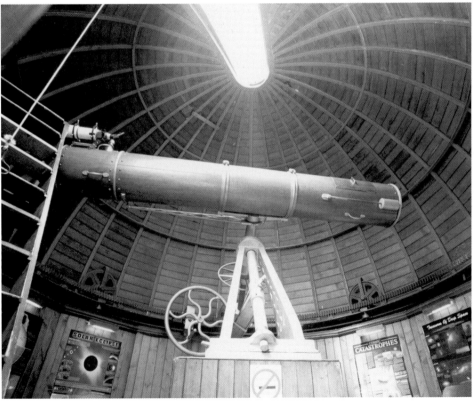

master was assisted by a Latin 'Doctor' and a Scots (later English) 'Doctor' who taught writing and arithmetic. Boys enrolled at eight and stayed for no more than five years. Thomas Buchannan, nephew of the more famous George, was master from 1571 to 1578 and one of his pupils, Robert Rollock, became the first principal of the new University of Edinburgh in 1592. When James VI and I returned to Scotland in 1617 he took part in a great debate and professed himself so pleased with the Latin oratory and the then master, one William Wallace, that he announced the founding of a 'free college' in Stirling. This promise failed to materialise until the University of Stirling was founded some 350 years later. The council built a new two-storey slate-roofed building in 1633, paying the master's salary partly from fees and partly from legacies such as that of John Cowane. As the school roll grew in the eighteenth century the council separated off the English (Writing and Arithmetic) School in 1740, which became independent in 1747. Later, the English School divided and a separate building opened in Baxter's Wynd (now Baker Street). The four official burgh schools moved about to cope with expansion until 1787 when the Guildry and (not to be outdone) the Seven Trades jointly funded a two-storey building on the former Greyfriars Yard where the High School now stands in Academy Road but a much smaller place. The ground floor housed the English School and the upper storey Writing and Arithmetic. The next year the council built the third and last grammar school on the Castle Hill site, designed by Gideon Gray, and it remained as this until 1856. Now it is a pub and restaurant called The Portcullis.

The rector during the late eighteenth century was Dr David Doig, a noted scholar and author of several articles in the *Encyclopaedia Britannica*. Robert Burns considered Doig 'a queerish figure and something of a pedant', as he wrote after taking supper with him on 27 August 1787.

By the mid-nineteenth century the Old Grammar School was in the care of George Munro, a brilliant scholar but a completely inept headmaster. It attracted very few pupils and everyone wanted Munro to resign; one of his assistants even set up a rival school. Despite all of this, he refused to retire and he died in harness in 1853.

By that time there were plans to build a new school, thanks to a former pupil, Colonel Tennant, who donated £1,000, and further financial input from the town council. The West Wing was erected on the Greyfriars Yard site and the existing English and Writing Schools were demolished to make way. Initially, the West Wing was entered from Academy Road via an imposing arch under a central tower. To the north and south of the entrance stretched two huge classrooms, each with a large stone fireplace. That on the left housed Mathematics, that on the right, English. At either end were two-storey buildings, to the north, a gymnasium with an art room above it; to the south, a modern language 'school' on the ground floor with the Classics room upstairs. It was a great success, both academically and as a building, and remained under town-council stewardship until it joined the Scottish Education system in the wake of the 1872 Education Act. The wing on Spittal Street was designed by another former pupil, the noted architect J. Marjoribanks MacLaren, in about 1888 and provided a new library and other facilities, the most notable being an astronomical observatory built using a donation from Sir Henry Campbell Bannerman MP, later Prime Minister. However, by the 1960s the 1,100 pupils were outgrowing the building and it lacked decent sports facilities. A new building at Torbrex was constructed and 'The School on the Rock' closed for good. It later accommodated the school library service, burgh archives and other council offices; eventually it became the Stirling Highland Hotel.

The Coming of the Railways

'We're a' ruined noo, we're a' ruined noo, the Iron Horse is comin' an' it's runnin' through an' through.' According to a ninety-year-old man, J.W. Campbell, in the centenary edition of the *Stirling Observer* (1936) this was a popular chant at about the time trains first came to Stirling. Clearly the attitudes to the coming of the railway were somewhat ambivalent. The railway also spawned a thriving tourist industry, which expanded further as a result of Queen Victoria's fondness for nearby Braemar and Royal Deeside. Royal visits apart, it was the coming of the railways in the 1840s that changed the burgh more than at any other single period and created the town we see today.

In 1848 the Scottish Central Railway opened a service between Perth and Greenhill, which was the first through link between central Scotland and the north, and was an immediate success. Trains ran from Carlisle, Glasgow and Edinburgh to Greenhill, then north via Larbert, Plean, Bannockburn, Stirling, Bridge of Allan and Dunblane, then north-east to Crieff Junction and Forteviot and thence to Perth. This line is still used and Perth remains the

Callander railway station, 1886. The continued reliance on horse-drawn transport for onward journeys is very apparent in this photograph. (*SCLS*)

The glory of steam! This train is passing the Stirling Middle signal-box, opened in 1901 by the Caledonian Railway. It had the distinction, until 2000, of having the last lower-quadrant signal. (*Stirling Council*)

junction for Aberdeen and Inverness. The line to Aberdeen through Strathmore is closed but the route via Dundee is still open.

In 1850 the new stone-built four-road Stirling Locomotive Shed opened, replacing a timber building left over from the work of the contractors, for freight locomotives and the Callander & Oban Railway. Another line, the Stirling & Dunfermline Railway, arrived that year, travelling west via Alloa with a branch to Alloa harbour for passengers travelling to Stirling by boat. In 1853 a bridge was constructed across the Forth and the line extended to Stirling, with a station built beside that of the Scottish Central Railway. In 1854 work began on the Forth & Clyde Railway between Stirling and Balloch on Loch Lomond and later to Glasgow, with the first sod cut by the Duke of Montrose at Cowane's Hospital Park. Many trains stopped at farms and hamlets, which were in real danger of becoming isolated since the railways had all but killed off horse-bus traffic. There was then a period of rationalisation and take-overs, with the North British and the Caledonian Railways emerging predominant. The Caledonian blithely assumed the royal arms of Scotland as its crest, but perhaps with justification. The upshot for Stirling was two-fold. The first was an increase in 'pleasure' traffic through the burgh – for instance, when the foundation stone of the Wallace Monument was laid in 1861 an estimated 15,000 visitors arrived by rail alone in many specially laid-on trains. The second was the possibility that Stirling could be a commuter base for Edinburgh and Glasgow, leading to an upsurge in new house building.

Another result of the railway, apart from tourism, was an influx of further residents. New Victorian suburbs appeared as merchants and businessmen from Glasgow flocked to the town, attracted by the scenery and the ease of commuting to the city just 25 miles away. They also brought with them something Glasgow had nurtured for years but which had been absent from the old Stirling – a desire to demonstrate civic pride manifested in the erection of amenities and municipal grandeur. Sadly, no philanthropic giant of industry, no Carnegie, Nairn or Burrell came forward, so it has always been the town council and local ratepayers who have borne the cost of schools, hospitals, bridges, the courthouse, places of edification and amusement, shopping galleries, public halls, water reservoirs and civic buildings. The Old Town Gaol is a case in point, which was built in the 1840s to replace the facilities in the Tolbooth which were universally considered to be among the worst in Scotland. Even the Wallace Monument was built by public subscription. But the town developed nonetheless and may be the better for it. Many a Scottish burgh has some unsustainable folly or wrongly placed park inspired by a rich local worthy and accepted by a council too polite to turn it down.

Stirling, by contrast, has a number of excellent and distinctive buildings from the nineteenth century, all functional and all in keeping with the overall look and feel of the town. Among the best are the Albert Halls, the Stirling Smith Art Gallery and Museum and the many architectural works of Alexander Bowie, as well as the commercial buildings at the Alhambra and the Arcade.

The Albert Halls opened in 1883 with Handel's *Messiah* and thereafter staged the usual programmes of light operetta and dramatic performances. The statue of Robert Burns stands guard across the road. (*Stirling Council*)

Old Town Gaol

The Old Town Gaol at the top of St John Street was opened in 1847. For the previous four centuries, prisoners had been kept in the Tolbooth, such an overcrowded and insanitary place that it was roundly condemned in 1842 as the worst in Scotland. The inspector of prisons had severely criticised the gaol after his visit six years earlier on 24 November 1836:

> I had heard a bad account of the Stirling Gaol from two or three quarters before visiting it, and my examination fully justified these unfavourable reports. The prison, nevertheless, is not an old one having been built more than 30 years. Great ignorance, however, of all the legitimate objects of imprisonment is manifest both in the choice of site and in the construction of the building. The prison is placed in so public a situation that it would be almost impossible to prevent communication from without; an object indeed which does not seem to have entered the heads of those who made the plans. The masonry, too, is so bad that holes can be easily made through the walls; so that, even security, the most evident of all requisites in a prison has not been attained or apparently cared for. As to the reform of the offender, that is quite out of the question; nay, it is hopeless to try to prevent his becoming worse. It would not be safe to set him to work, lest he should employ his tools in making his way through the frail tenement in which he is confined; and so insufficient are the means of separation, that all the females, of whom there are sometimes 12 or 15 at one time, are huddled together in the same room. In the absence of the keeper, too, who does not reside on the spot, conversation can readily be kept up between the females and the males; and about 12 months ago one of the females bored a hole through the wall into the adjoining males' cell, to render the communication easier.

Prison reform was on the Victorian agenda, so a new purpose-built gaol was required. Designed by Thomas Brown, it incorporated the improvements promoted by William Brebner, noted reformer and Governor of Glasgow's Bridewell: one prisoner per cell, inclusion of a work and education programme, washing areas, food provided and Stirling's first central-heating system. It was originally the county gaol but from 1888 (when County Prison Boards were abolished in favour of a centralised system) to 1935 it was used as the only military prison in Scotland and afterwards as the civil defence headquarters and training centre. The gaol reverted to the council ownership and was sold in 1955 to the first of a series of private developers. However, no one managed to come up with a viable new scheme for the building and it fell into disrepair. In 1985 it was re-acquired by the council and in the early 1990s was restored as a visitor attraction, providing a 'living history' experience of what life was like behind bars in the nineteenth century. A notable feature is the re-created stocks, outside the gaol, which has spaces for an odd number of legs. The original stocks were actually kept in the Tolbooth and brought out when needed. In fact, they were only used a handful of times between their introduction in the 1500s and their abandonment in the 1730s, and usually for infractions such as insulting one's social superiors, failing to pay a fine for swearing, idleness, poaching, non-observance of the Sabbath and similar serious crimes against the fragile fabric of society. Stirling's modern prison, the all-female Corton Vale prison, is a far cry from those unenlightened days.

Victorian Splendour

Many of Stirling's finest thoroughfares are lined with the results of the Victorian building boom. But beyond the grand former banks and arcades there are other reminders of the productive nineteenth century.

The Victorians went to some lengths to provide 'improving' and inspirational monuments in the town, even when these had no direct relationship with Stirling. A good example is the Valley Cemetery where a memorial was erected to the Wigtown Martyrs. This commemorates Margaret Wilson of Wigtown (near Dumfries) who was drowned aged eighteen (along with her sister Agnes, thirteen, and Margaret McLachlan, an elderly woman in her sixties) for refusing to renounce the Protestant faith. This was in May 1685, when suppression of Covenanters was at its height. The story tells that the women were betrayed by an informer, Patrick Stuart, when they refused to drink the king's health. They spent a month in prison, were tried as rebels

King Street, seen here ably protected by one of Stirling's finest in the early twentieth century. At this time it boasted many impressive Victorian buildings and shops. The Crawford Arcade is near the top right and most of the banks are now bars. (*SCLS*)

The crowning glory of King Street, the 'Royal Way', is The Steeple or Athenaeum, designed by William Stirling of Dunblane in the image of a classical gentlemen's club. Built in 1816 it had a library, public rooms and two shops on the ground floor (now a florist and a jeweller). The tall, six-stage square tower and spire is fronted by a portico which was constructed in 1859 and supports 'The Wee Wallace', a statue of William Wallace by Handyside Ritchie. Charles Rogers, the main organiser of the Wallace Monument, bought it, persuaded a local businessman to pay and talked the council into having it erected. Until 1840 King Street was called Quality Street. (*Stirling Council*)

Murray Place runs into Barnton Street which carries on north towards the Old Bridge. Murray Place was built to connect Stevenson's new bridge with King Street and set the seal on the process by which the focus of Stirling moved from Broad Street and the Mercat Cross to the lower part of the town. (*Stirling Council*)

Running the other way from King Street is Port Street. At the intersection seen in the photograph above, the elegant building on the left is, predictably, a burger bar. The photograph below shows the continuation of Port Street across Dumbarton Road. Both postcards date from the 1930s. (*SCLS*)

and were sentenced to death by drowning in Wigtown Bay. There is some controversy over the details – it may not actually have happened. Victorian sensibilities declared that the monument itself should completely ignore the facts of the case and present a somewhat idealised depiction of women's suffering.

Stirling also has the Victorian era to thank for the Smith Art Gallery and Museum, probably one of the best-kept secrets in Scotland. It sits unobtrusively under Stirling Castle rock in the King's Park, previously the hunting grounds of the Stuart monarchs, now Albert Place, a leafy suburb of Victorian mansions. 'The Smith' was founded in 1874 from the bequest of the artist Thomas Stuart Smith who died in 1869. Stirling and its surrounding area of great scenic beauty attracted many artists, especially in the aftermath of Sir Walter Scott's popularisation of the region and the restriction on foreign travel imposed during the Peninsular War and the Crimea hostilities. The original Smith collections are the nucleus of a remarkable compilation of over 1,000 watercolours, oils, drawings, prints and etchings. Included in these are a remarkable set of Scottish paintings, with works by John Duncan, Sir William Allan and Alexander Nasmyth, as well as seventy-four sketches of Stirling people by local boy Sir George Harvey PRSA (1806–76), which he later used in his great Scottish history paintings.

For many years Joseph Denovan Adam (1841–96), best known as a painter of dogs and puppies and bucolic Highland landscapes, had Scotland's only school of animal painting and kept his own herd of Highland cattle and other beasts for students to paint. Today, artists like Steven Campbell live and work there.

'The Ladies' – Stirling's memorial to the Wigtown Martyrs. (*BD*)

Stirling's Carnegie Library and council buildings. (*SCLS*)

The Stirling Smith Art Gallery and Museum. Now part funded by Stirling Council, the Smith has a £3 million extension programme under way. (*Stirling Council*)

A painting by Joseph Denovan Adam (1841–96). He featured homely scenes and landscapes in his work, and even kept his own Highland cattle who also served as subjects. (*Stirling Smith Art Gallery and Museum*)

The portrait collection contains many famous figures, from the expected William Wallace, Robert Bruce, Mary, Queen of Scots and Bonnie Prince Charlie and a previously unknown portrait of Robert Burns, to the less familiar, such as composer Arcangelo Corelli (1653–1713), a near-contemporary of Purcell, Vivaldi, Handel and Bach. Corelli, populariser of the Concerto Grosso principle, had a profound influence on Scottish music for a generation. Local musicians such as William McGibbon (1696–1756) produced many works in imitation of Corelli, including six trio sonatas and a set of 'graces' (ornaments) to one of Corelli's solo violin sonatas.

The Smith must be the only museum and gallery in the world whose External Relations Officer is a Highland bull. Hamish, the Smith's 'publicity coo', arrived in 1996 for a Joseph Denovan Adam exhibition. He and his little brother Hector, as well as an entourage of sheep and goats, stayed in the Smith grounds during the summer to the delight of visitors.

The museum also has one of the most important and least known Scottish history collections. Remarkable pieces include: the world's oldest football, the earliest dated curling stone (1511) in the world; the Stirling Jug of 1457, the measure by which all other Scottish measures were regulated; ancient tartans, woven in Wilson's mills in Bannockburn; a good collection of sculpture dating from about 1670 to the present; and a figure of Justice originally from the Tolbooth. This rendition pre-dates the traditional blindfold, used from the sixteenth century onwards. The Smith's Justice statue must have seen many famous trials including that of the radicals Baird and Hardie, sentenced to death for their part in the 1820 rising. The executioner's cloak and axe are also in the Smith.

The museum has a significant collection of Scottish weapons. Stirling is rightly famous as the site of six battles that changed the course of Scottish history – 'To hold Stirling is to hold Scotland' – so it is not surprising that the town was famous for its swordsmiths, as nearby Doune was renowned for its pistol making. Many of the old cattle drove roads merged at Stirling, so there is a significant collection of leather goods, horn utensils and ancient charm stones used to cure cattle diseases.

The museum also houses Jacobite memorabilia, medieval pottery, Renaissance furniture and artifacts from the Seven Trades of Stirling – bakers, butchers, tailors, cordwainers (shoe makers), skinners, hammermen (blacksmiths) and weavers – as well as archaeological finds from around the district, and an excellent botanical, geological and natural history collection.

Robert Burns – Almost the Stirlingshire Bard

It is completely justifiable for Stirling to lay some claim to Robert Burns and to have a statue of the great man. Apart from his supreme national importance, he was a frequent visitor to Stirling, drew inspiration at Bannockburn for his most lasting song ('Scots Wha' Hae' – the Scots national anthem in all but name), left some libellous anti-monarchy sentiments scratched on the window of an inn and would probably have ended up living nearby had he survived past his all-too-short thirty-eight years.

Robert Burns stands facing Bannockburn and with his back resolutely and appropriately turned against the neighbouring statue of Henry Campbell Bannerman, whose politics he would have despised. He may well be remembering Stirling's first Burns Supper at the Wingate Inn in King Street, which the poet himself attended in 1787, just before his untimely death. The statue was gifted by Provost David Bayne in 1914, who also gave the clock in Wallace Street. (*Stirling Council*)

Burns was travelling with his friend, Willie Nicol, an Edinburgh schoolmaster, in August 1787. They visited the tomb of Sir John de Graham and Camelon, then proceeded to Carron to see the famous ironworks. They were refused admission – not surprising as it was a Sunday – so Burns resorted to scratching his displeasure – and his version of Blake's 'dark satanic mills' – on a window-pane of the inn at Carron with a diamond:

> We cam na here to view your warks,
>   In hopes to be mair wise,
> But only, lest we gang to hell,
>   It may be nae surprise:
> But when we tirl'd at your door
>   Your porter dought na hear us;
> Sae may, shou'd we to Hell's yetts come,
>   Your billy Satan sair us!

Full marks, though, go to a Mr Benson, a traveller for the Carron company, who copied Burns' lines into his order book followed by this reply – bear in mind that Burns had tried to enter incognito.

> If you came here to see our works,
> You should have been more civil,
> Than give us a fictitious name,
> In hopes to cheat the devil.
>
> Six days a-week to you and all,
> We think it very well;
> The other, if you go to church,
> May keep you out of hell.

So there!

Burns and Nicol also took lunch at Auchenbowie House then visited Bannockburn where they saw the house in which James III was murdered. Burns was impressed by the battlefield and the Borestone where Robert Bruce had planted his standard. 'I said a fervent prayer for Old Caledonia over the hole in a blue whinstone, where Robert de Bruce fixed his royal standard . . .' he wrote later.

As was usual on his tours, Burns also collected local tunes and fragments of verse for his own use. He heard many old Scottish melodies, including (according to tradition) the battle march of Bruce's men at Bannockburn which would later become 'Scots Wha' Hae'. Burns's empathy with the radical principles of the French Republic of 1793 ('Liberté, Egalité et Fraternité') spurred him to write this battle-hymn which he sent, set to 'Hey Tuttie Taittie', to Thomson in 1794. Thomson hated the tune and almost talked Burns out of using it. It was finally published in 1799. Sometimes subtitled 'Robert Bruce's March to Bannockburn', the song has since become synonymous with Scottish freedom and independence from England. 'There is a tradition', Burns wrote later in a letter to his old friend George Thomson 'that the old air "Hey Tuttie Taittie" was Robert Bruce's march at the battle of Bannockburn. This thought, in my solitary wanderings, has warmed me to a pitch of enthusiasm on the theme of liberty and independence which I have thrown into a kind of Scottish ode, fitted to the air, that one might suppose to be the gallant Scot's address to his heroic followers on that eventful morning.'

This was more than sentimental poetry: it was effectively rabble-rousing. Burns puts into the mouth of a follower of Robert Bruce a song of freedom that was still being sought in the Scotland of his day. On 1 February 1793 the French Republic had declared war on Britain. The Hanoverian government responded by suppressing the Friends of the People, the radical movement organised by a young lawyer, Thomas Muir of Huntershill, who was tried for treason on 30 August, the date Burns sent the song to Thomson, and was sentenced to fourteen years' transportation. Burns agreed to let the *Morning Chronicle* publish 'Scots Wha' Hae' on 8 May 1794 provided they 'insert it as a thing they have met with by accident, and unknown to me'. Had he declared his seditous sympathies more openly he might have been arrested and tried like Muir. Robert Burns's 'Scots Wha' Hae':

> Scots, wha hae wi Wallace bled,
> Scots, wham Bruce has aften led,
> Welcome to your gory bed
>   Or to victorie!
> Now's the day, and now's the hour:
> See the front o' battle lour,
> See approach proud Edward's power –
>   Chains and slaverie!
>
> Wha will be a traitor knave?
> Wha can fill a coward's grave?
> Wha sae base as be a slave? –
>   Let him turn and flee!
> Wha for Scotland's King and Law
> Freedom's sword will strongly draw,
> Freeman stand, or Freeman fa',
>   Let him follow me!
>
> By Oppression's woes and pains,
> By your sons in servile chains,
> We will drain your dearest veins,
>   But they shall be free!
> Lay the proud usurpers low!
> Tyrants fall in every foe!
> Liberty's in every blow!
>   Let us do, or die!

When the National Wallace Monument opened a Hall of Heroes, the bust of Robert Burns was the first to be installed. The unveiling was accompanied by the singing of 'Scots Wha' Hae', as had the laying of the monument's foundation stone.

Scratchings on Windows

Stirred by his visits to Bannockburn and Stirling, Burns was prompted to other seditious scribbling. On several occasions he was moved to scratch poems on windows of inns with a diamond: his rather unjustified complaint at the inn at Carron, a sentimental quatrain at the Cross Keys Inn, Falkirk, where he and Nicol started their tour of the north on 25 August 1787, and again two days later in Stirling and at least one other.

During his journey with Nicol, they stayed at Wingate's Inn in Quality Street (renamed King Street), now the Golden Lion Hotel. Nicol awoke on 27 August 1787 to find this poem inscribed on the window-pane:

The Golden Lion, scene of Robert Burns's fenestral poetry. (*SCLS*)

This 1900s postcard shows the Gathering Stone at Sherrifmuir, which may have inspired Burns to write the ballad 'The Battle of Sherra-Moor [Sherrifmuir]'. (*BD*)

> Here Stuarts once in glory reigned,
> And laws for Scotland's weal ordained;
> But now unroof'd their palace stands,
> Their sceptre's sway'd by other hands;
> Fallen indeed, and to the earth
> Whence groveling reptiles take their birth.
> The injured Stuart line is gone,
> A race outlandish fills their throne;
> An idiot race, to honour lost;
> Who knows them best despise them most.

These powerful thoughts were prompted by Burns's distress at seeing the ruined state of Stirling Castle and the Great Hall where the Scottish Parliament had met and doubtless also by his emotions at Bannockburn. Nicol cautioned Burns against leaving such an obvious anti-Hanoverian slander, particularly at a sensitive time when the government was cracking down on dissent, especially in Scotland. Burns responded by adding the following qualifier as a reproof to the 'anonymous' author:

> Rash mortal, and slanderous Poet! Thy name
> Shall no longer appear in the records of fame;
> Dost not know that old Mansfield, who writes like the Bible,
> Says – the more 'tis a truth, sir, the more 'tis a libel?

Burns went further some two months later. It is said that he returned to the inn and smashed the glass with his riding crop. (Another version has the famous window-pane lost in a fire at the inn.) But the real damage had been done – many travellers had copied the epigram and it was widely circulated. It was particularly timely as the Young Pretender, Bonnie Prince Charlie, died in exile in Rome, a dissolute alcoholic, in January 1788. This effectively ended any hopes for a Stuart challenge to the Hanoverian rule. There was a fair amount of debate at the time as to whether Burns (or perhaps Nicol) was the author. Burns himself recorded the poem in his collection of manuscripts, coyly entitling it 'Wrote by Somebody in an Inn at Stirling On Seeing the Royal Palace in Ruin (1787)', but he admitted to its authorship in a letter to 'Clarinda', a lady he wrote to frequently, a few months later. It was well known and later almost cost him his job as an excise collector.

In Stirling, Burns also picked up the chorus of 'My Harry was a Gallant Gay' – a tune long connected to the 42nd regiment (the Black Watch) – from an old woman in Dunblane and added the verses. He also wrote 'The Battle of Sherra-Moor' (Sherrifmuir), a paraphrasing of the Revd John Barclay's earlier ballad, which includes the description of the Redcoats pursued to Stirling and denied access during the Jacobite rising of 1715, also known as Mar's Rebellion:

> I saw mysel, they did pursue,
> The horsemen back to Forth, man;

And at Dunblane, in my ain sight,
They took the brig wi' a' their might,
And straught to Stirling wing'd their flight;
But, cursed lot! the gates were shut.

Robert Burns's last song, 'Fairest maid on Devon banks, Crystal Devon, winding Devon', was written in July 1796 nine days before his death. It refers to Charlotte Hamilton of Mauchline whom he had met at nearby Harviestoun nine years before during his visit to Bannockburn and Stirling. She was also the subject of an earlier poem in 1787, 'The Banks of the Devon'. The water of the Devon was used for textile mills and bleachfields in the eighteenth and nineteenth centuries, mostly by entrepreneurs from Dunfermline, a major weaving centre at the time. The Devon takes a winding course to join the Forth at Alloa and the Falls of Devon are a noted beauty spot. Nearby is Crook of Devon, a village famous in the seventeenth century for cattle fairs and witch burnings. Crook of Devon is 'Twinned with Thief of Baghdad', as the local joke has it.

Dunblane and Stirling have a further connection with Burns. Working as an excise collector in Dumfries, he was put forward for promotion as supervisor at Dunblane, to start in August 1797. Burns would undoubtedly have got the post, but he died in the July of the previous year. Given his increased salary and reduced workload (at the time he was trying to run a farm and also travel 200 miles a week on his excise duties), Burns would no doubt have been able to devote more time to his writing and would have left an even larger and greater corpus of works. He might then have been known as the 'Stirlingshire Bard' and forever associated with the area, rather than with Ayrshire.

Stirling Castle dominates the townscape – although Holy Rude, the Tolbooth and the old High School Observatory are prominent – but the surrounding hills make it clear why Stirling is described as 'A huge brooch, clasping Highlands and Lowlands together', Alexander Smith, 1856. *(John McPake, Stirling Council)*

John Betjeman advised us to walk around our towns looking up at the first storeys. Stirling has an eclectic wealth of interesting building features reflecting the whole of Scotland's architecture – the crow-stepped gables on the right, the six-stage square tower and spire in 1859 and the 1816 Athenaeum, seen above, and the classically inspired frontages of adjoining King Street seen below. (*John McPake, Stirling Council*)

Stirling isn't short of impressive statuary. Some of it is hard to miss – like the statues of Burns and Bannerman or the protective presence of William Wallace in the portico fronting the Athenaeum, the Golden Lion (above) and 'Staneybreeks' (John Cowane). But some is rarely noticed, even the statue of Mary, Queen of Scots (right) adorning the top of the municipal buildings. (*John McPake, Stirling Council*)

The Cock and the Clock. The sympathetic but bold transformation of the Tolbooth into an arts venue and restaurant is both a lynch pin and a symbol of Stirling's avowal to combine the best of the past with the needs of the present while avoiding sterile 'conservation' of buildings purely for their own sake – as if our forebears who built them would ever have accorded them the same respect. The marriage of old and new is particularly well expressed in the foyer and the staircase (below). (*John McPake, Stirling Council*)

If Stirling is the doorway to the
Highlands, Stirling's own
doorways are no less romantic
and inspiring. The small selection
seen on this page and opposite
reveal the colour and variety that
will be seen during a walk
around the city. The doors seen
above and below are found in
Princes Street. The fanlight seen
above opposite is from Allan
Park. Bothwell House is in fact
the door to Auchenbowie's
House. (*John McPake, Stirling
Council*)

A selection from the wealth of architectural detail found on buildings around the city is seen here and opposite. The photograph below is of Erskine's crest on Mar's Wark. The faces of Bruce, Wallace, Burns and other luminaries, as well as cherubs, angels and figures from myth and legend, peer down from many buildings and monuments. (*John McPake, Stirling Council*)

The roofscape shows the structure of the Top of the Town as it evolved over the centuries, from the medieval houses and the castle at the top down St John Street on the left and Broad Street to the right. (*John McPake, Stirling Council*)

The contrast of older housing with newer building can be seen here. The centre of the city has undergone significant changes and the spread outwith the city walls has extended Stirling on all sides. (*John McPake, Stirling Council*)

Monument to Ebenezer Erskine (1680–1745). By 1733 an act of 1712 that had removed the democratic right of congregations to choose their own ministers had caused such popular resentment that a group of ministers left to set up the Original Secession Church. One of their leaders was Ebenezer Erskine, third minister in Stirling. The congregation gathered at a meeting house in the garden of a house in St John Street (then known as Back Raw). In about 1820 they sold this and used the money to commission Allan Johnstone as architect of the new building seen above. When Erskine died he was laid to rest in a grave beside the altar of the original church and in 1859 the site was marked with the monument in the foreground. The next year the name Erskine Church was formally adopted and in 1934 the congregation merged with that of Marykirk, and the church has been known as Erskine Marykirk ever since. It was almost totally destroyed by fire and became derelict. In 1994 Stirling Council demolished the building but retained the imposing façade and incorporated it into what is now a youth centre. (*John McPake, Stirling Council*)

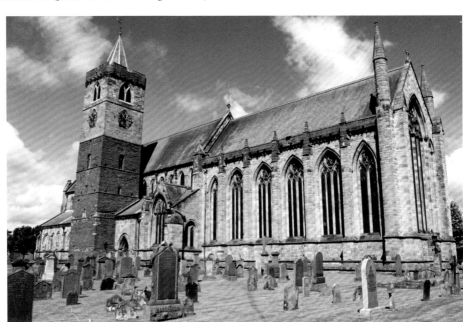

Dunblane Cathedral (although there are technically no cathedrals in the Church of Scotland) is a mere 5 miles from Stirling. It was built in the thirteenth century on the site of St Blane's fifth-century Celtic church. (*John McPake, Stirling Council*)

Among Holy Rude's treasures are magnificent stained glass, both ancient and modern, the unique medieval open timber roof and the largest church organ in Scotland. Note the Guildry ring seen in the window above. (*John McPake, Stirling Council*)

ST

JOHN

Many of Stirling's buildings – especially the public ones – have impressive interior features from cornicing and fireplaces to staircases and panels. A room at Airthrey Castle is seen above. The plasterwork and staircase below are found in the Viewforth building. (*John McPake, Stirling Council*)

Too often it happens in our towns and cities that new retail developments drive out older businesses and historic streets become deserted and forlorn. Stirling manages to accommodate both, with modern constructions like the Thistle Centre and redevelopments of Victorian arcades like the Crawford (above) sitting happily alongside the traditional. Murray Place (below) retains human-scale charm and small shops. (*John McPake, Stirling Council*)

And, of course, a city wouldn't be a city without its theme café-bars, the discos, the occasional manic street entertainer (seen here in Friar's Street) and traditional back greens for the washing, such as Kelly Court seen below. Cities are built of stone, but they are composed of people. A great city is one where neither is sacrificed to the needs of the other. It's not easy, but Stirling manages better than many. (*John McPake, Stirling Council*)

5

Guilds, Trades & Industry

It is fair to say that for centuries Stirling's main industry was just being there. At least six battles were fought nearby which changed or shaped the course of British history. All of these were for possession of the castle, which commanded the only practical crossing of the River Forth and the boggy marshes to the west which prevented armies moving north or south. This naturally made Stirling a royal residence, as the castle was a safe haven for the monarchs of the day. And this in turn provided the rationale for a town to support the needs of the many courtiers, functionaries and soldiers who surrounded the sovereign. Like any thriving community, Stirling always had people who made things and people who sold things. Originally these would have been one and the same, but the growing influence of feudal ideas suggested a separation between craft and trade. As the site of a royal palace, Stirling would naturally have had a coterie of candlemakers, brewers, fleshers, carpenters, masons and all the other trades necessary to keep a large household and its courtiers well provided for. It would also be important for goods to be brought in – wines, spices, cloths and all manner of regal luxuries. In addition, the kings would wish to tax or levy such activities to provide much-needed revenue, hence the idea of royal burghs and guilds came about.

Burgh and Guildry

The influence of Queen Margaret and her Anglo-Norman court of 'illustrious exiles' had seen a growing influx of English and continental ideas and of feudal nobles being given lands in Scotland. Her sons, Edgar, Alexander I and David I, were well aware of these initiatives and their benefits. The reorganisation was confined at first to ecclesiastical matters, but gradually affected all sectors of Scottish life. Celtic religious orders were suppressed, English clerics replaced Scottish monks, new monasteries were founded and the Celtic Church was remodelled along Roman Catholic lines. Norman French overtook Gaelic at court, while English was increasingly spoken in the Borders and Lowlands. The traditional system of clan land tenure was abolished by David I. Claiming royal ownership of the land, he transferred large tracts to Anglo-Norman and Scottish nobles, who then became vassals of the Crown. David also introduced legislative and administrative reforms based on English models and encouraged commerce with England. Out of this the concepts of burghs and guilds arose.

The Guildry of Stirling was established by a royal charter of Alexander II in 1226, although the date of institution as recorded on the Guildry stamp is 1119. This is because the Guildry Charter was a formalisation of part of the Laws of the Four Burghs – Edinburgh, Roxburgh, Berwick and Stirling – which dated back more than a century to the reign of David I. He had given the town royal burgh status in 1124, granting the right to hold fairs and levy duties and establishing it as one of the most important towns and market-places of medieval Scotland.

The guilds must have existed before 1226 and possibly before 1124, as they were incorporated into the burgh. Based on the feudal set-up of Berwick (the first burgh) the laws regulated, for instance, who could become a burgess – essentially any merchant or craftsman with property within its boundaries, for which they paid a levy to the king. Burgesses had important privileges, not least being able to exclude non-burgh merchants and the right to buy and sell imports and goods such as hides and wool. But Alexander's charter went further, and states that: 'We grant also to our said burgesses of Strivelyn that they shall have a merchant gild, except the walkers and weavers.' It delineated who could take on apprentices, hire servants, engage in certain

On high days and public occasions the magistrates and town council would parade, preceded by a drummer and four town officers. This 1890s illustration shows the traditional sword and halberd, coat, vest, knee breeches, white hose and buckled shoes of a Guildry officer, whose coat, breeches and vest were green. The trades officer's was dark-blue with a red facing. (*BD*)

The Guildry symbol, a reversed figure four, was adopted from the merchants' mark, which can be found on headstones in the Valley Cemetery and elsewhere. The example seen here was carved on a chair. (*Stirling Council*)

activities and the like. For instance, no one could be a guild member if he worked with his own hands – he had to have employees or others to do so. This effectively created a distinction between those who made (craftsmen) and those who sold (merchants) and put control of the burgh in the hands of the sellers, rather than the producers.

Equally, the function of the Guildry was to regulate trade rather than manufacture. It had the beneficial effect of protectionism as no merchant from outside the burgh could trade at Stirling's weekly market. Guildry members dealt wholesale within the town and abroad, invested in shipping ventures, lent funds and acted as factors and agents. The 1226 charter also gave the merchants unrivalled power and influence. Not only was the Guildry's status almost the same as that of the town council, members were also in the majority on the town council itself. The Guildry Courts guarded its members' privileges and vigorously enforced them, and the town council was effectively a puppet. As one of the 'Curia Quatuor Burgorum' (Court of Four Burghs) – a sort of mercantile parliament, which could settle any legal or administrative issue relating to the Scottish burghs and their burgesses – Stirling took part in assizes held by the chamberlain, based at Haddington. These were convened with one burgess from each of the burghs of Edinburgh, Stirling, Berwick and Roxburgh (or when Berwick and Roxburgh were in English hands, Lanark and Linlithgow). Under the Laws of the Four Burghs the guild members were forbidden to manufacture anything, but they were in effective control of anything that could be bought or sold. Later this led to conflicts between the guilds and the crafts, who felt excluded from all commercial decision-making and the conduct of the town's affairs.

It should be realised that in the early medieval period, up to about 1300 (roughly the time of English incursions, the interregum and the battles of Wallace and Bruce), Scotland was a fairly prosperous country. It was one of the greatest producers of wool in Europe, possibly second only to England, ten times its size. Although most of this was controlled by the abbeys, the general benefits from the wealth generated trickled down to other members of the populace. Great cathedrals were built at St Andrews and Glasgow, abbeys at Dryburgh, Dunkeld and Dunfermline, new towns were laid out including Crail with its innovative double market-street plan and royal castles were constructed at Edinburgh and, of course, Stirling. So there was employment, agriculture and a steady increase in population. The Stirling guilds were well placed to capitalise on this.

But the time of plenty was not to last. The long series of wars with England, where both sides regularly devastated the land to deny it to the other, also affected international trade. The loss of Berwick made Edinburgh more important as a port, at the expense of the other wool towns such as Inverness, Perth and Stirling. The focus shifted towards leather and hides. The poor harvests and famines of 1315 and the 1330s and the plagues of 1349 and 1361 took their toll. The currency had to be devalued – by 1400 the Pound Scots was worth 30 per cent of its value before 1296 and possibly as little as 12 per cent by 1500. By 1450 the Pound Scots was worth only a third that of its English counterpart and the relative scarcity of peasant labour forced a re-evaluation of the relationship between landowner and serf. The feudal system was becoming outdated, as rents dropped and tenants could demand better terms, bigger landholdings and generally fairer treatment. The net effect was increased importance of those who could do and make, as opposed to those who could merely control and sell. The crafts were on the up and up.

The Seven Incorporated Trades

Medieval society was very hierarchical, with strict demarcations based on rank, occupation and proximity to the nobility. The division between crafts (who merely made things) and merchants (who dealt with the palace and the buying and selling of goods) had been instigated in Alexander II's charter. Guilds were established by royal decree whereas crafts were recognised by 'Seals of Cause' issued by the town council. Stirling's merchants therefore tended to look down on the crafts or trades – a distinction between business and manufacture that, sadly, persists in today's society – even though a number of the manufacturers were every bit as rich as the merchants.

Different trades gathered in different parts of the burgh. Tanners and brewers needed plenty of running water for their businesses, so they lived close to the town burn, which now runs underground. Candlemakers and blacksmiths, who ran the risk of fire, and other trades using furnaces or kilns, set up shop at the bottom of the hill where an accident was less likely to burn down the whole town. They got their coal from pits at Bruce land at Auchenbowie near Bannockburn.

Most crafts had a governing body which laid down standards of work, conduct and training, set rules for its members, masters and apprentices and regulated prices and pay rates. The Trade Guild also protected the interests of the craftsmen.

In the fifteenth century, a number of Stirling's craft organisations banded together as the Seven Incorporated Trades in order to strengthen their hand. The interests of the guilds, it was felt, were not always in tune with those of the crafts. The guilds' hegemony over the burgh council, and therefore over prices, tariffs and markets, was felt to be excessive. The burgh council, as in most Scottish towns, controlled building, weights and measures, the strength of ale, market prices and policing and developed the harbour, the Tolbooth, the all-important bridges, markets and a grammar school. The influential merchants on the council created and controlled the burgh's wealth and used their town-council positions to pass by-laws favourable to trade and to regulate the prices of craft goods and sources of raw materials. The trades sought to challenge the predominance of the guilds and must have been thrilled when they received a royal charter from Mary, Queen of Scots in 1556 along with – it is said – the 'Blue Blanket', a banner made by her own hand and a copy of the one gifted to the Edinburgh Trades in 1460 by James III.

There was recognition for bakers, fleshers (butchers), tailors, cordwainers (shoe makers), skinners, hammermen (blacksmiths) and weavers. None for

The Flesher's Tavern in St John Street, typical of houses of its time and named for one of the trades, is shown in this early lithograph, unsigned and undated. It might be by Lindley Sambourne, who certainly made other drawings of it in 1876 or so. During demolition in the 1950s the building was found to have a wall painting showing the arrival of Mary, Queen of Scots from France. Auchenbowie's House at the Top of the Town retains a similar feature turret staircase to the one seen here; the Flesher's Tavern no longer exists. (*BD*)

brewers, notice, even though this was a popular, even essential, occupation and Stirling held the legal measure of the Scots pint. In fact, the maltmen were so powerful they were specifically excluded from the trades, as were masons and other wrights.

Also, anyone working directly for the castle was exempt as being outwith the burgh's jurisdiction – for example, Robert Spittal the royal tailor, was excused from joining the tailors' craft.

Just as each merchant guild had a dean, each craft was governed by a deacon, a treasurer and a clerk and had its own chapel in the Church of the Holy Rude. Churches then also served as meeting-places and business was conducted there. Guildhalls and craft lodges were a natural extension of this tradition, especially after the Reformation.

The Seven Incorporated Trades shared a common 'box' – a large chest where they kept their Blue Blanket and their joint funds – with seven locks, one for each craft. Each key was held by the 'boxman' (treasurer) of each craft and the chest could only be opened by common consent of all the crafts. More than anything else, this was a symbol of their solidarity.

The amalgamation of the trades was a success. The deacons secured the right to sit on the town council and the crafts challenged the dominance of the merchants. But it was hard-won and confrontation was inevitable, even occasionally violent. There was conflict over the ladle tax, by which the Stirling burgh demanded a ladleful of grain for each barrel brought to the market. In

JOHN COWANE

The name most associated with the development of the Guildry is John Cowane, a wealthy merchant who was twice elected the Dean between 1623 and 1633, served on the council for over twenty years and was a representative to the convention of royal burghs. He was also Stirling's main early philanthropist, endowing a hospital and leaving a great deal of land which is still held in trust for the relief of the poor and continues to play a role in the conservation and development of Stirling.

Cowane left 500 merks to the Church of the Holy Rude and an endowment of 40,000 merks for an alms house and the maintenance of thirteen elderly 'gildbreithers' (guild members who had fallen on hard times). The merk was ⅔ of a Pound Scots and equivalent to an English shilling. Cowane's Hospital, as it became known, was built beside the church sometime between 1638 and 1649. Apparently, it had strict house rules which were not popular with the residents. Originally a two-storey building, the main part was altered in 1852 to make a Guildhall where guilds met and held dinners. Later it became a schoolhouse and was used as a hospital during epidemics. Now it is mainly a venue for concerts, ceilidhs, medieval banquets and meetings. Inside there are portraits of past deans and it has a statue of John Cowane above the door, which is said to be a good likeness.

The statue of Cowane above the door. Known locally as 'Staneybreeks' ('stone trousers'), tradition has it that every Hogmanay he comes down for a dance. (*Stirling Council*)

A 1907 postcard showing John Cowane's Hospital, also known at that time as the Guildhall. (*BD*)

1613, the council accused the crafts of grain hoarding in order to push up prices as compensation for the ladles lost in tax. The merchants fought it in a rigged court and the bakers' leaders were gaoled in the Tolbooth. However, an ex-deacon of the skinners forced the gaoler to release them and the Seven Incorporated Trades rampaged through the burgh, armed to the teeth and spoiling for a fight. The Earl of Mar, hereditary Keeper of the Castle, felt a show of strength was required if order was to be restored. He had all the craft leaders arrested and gaoled in Edinburgh. The minister of the Church of the Holy Rude interceded for their release. This was not the last time the craftsmen of Stirling felt prepared to go to prison or even the gallows for their rights – some 200 years later the martyrs of the Radical Rebellion suffered a similar fate.

The Seven Incorporated Trades were not above employing protectionism to safeguard their own interests, just as the Guildry had done to them. The maltmen were considered a trade at the start of the sixteenth century and had a deacon. But the human appetite for fermented beverage being what it is, they became rich and therefore powerful and disruptive. In 1567 they were excluded from the trades by Act of Parliament. In 1603 James VI restored their privileges, but without the right to elect a deacon. Their chief officer – called the 'Visitor' – represented them. They were considered one of the four 'tolerated communities' within Stirling, alongside the mechanics (which included all masons, plasterers,

Robert Spittal's House, which was, in fact, no such thing. Spittal was tailor to James IV and in 1530 left money to help the poor of Stirling. The building seen here was erected in about 1650 using his endowments and was later divided into tenement flats. (*Stirling Council*)

The photograph shows the gravestone of a maltman, with the distinctive malt shovel. The Forth Valley was once a very important brewing area and supported over thirty-two breweries. This was a result of the port facilities, ample crop-growing fertile lands and fresh water from the Ochil Hills. Beers and ales from here were shipped throughout Scotland, to England and other parts of the world. Sadly there are no longer any large breweries left in the area but brewing still continues in the Forth Valley thanks to the four local micro breweries, like Bridge of Allan which produces fine-quality Scottish ales and still exports overseas. (*Stirling Council*)

slaters, painters, coopers, dyers and others), the barbers and periwigmakers, the *omnium gatherum* (manual workers and others who could not join any other guild or craft) and, briefly after 1726, the chapmen.

The Eighteenth Century and the Industrial Revolution

Following the departure of the royal court in 1603 when James VI became King of England, Stirling looked to prosper through the business activities of its merchants and the burgh council. Forced to look beyond the castle for their trade, Stirling's industries – mostly based on water, such as weaving, tanning and brewing – developed strong links and trade routes via the River Forth with Holland and Scandinavia. However, the seventeenth century brought bad fortune to the local economy. Plague broke out in 1645, and famine in 1695. A further setback was the collapse of the Company of Scotland Trading to Africa, taking with it large investments by the town council and several merchants. In 1714, trade was disrupted by the Battle of Sherrifmuir which discouraged visitors to the burgh.

These factors helped to prevent any major advance in the economy of the region until the Industrial Revolution reached Stirling in the late eighteenth century. Before this, the region had a well-established diversity of trades and crafts but there were probably more people involved in hand spinning and weaving than any other occupation. Craftspeople lived and worked in their homes. In the countryside, this situation continued well into the nineteenth century. The natural benefits of Stirling's position made it a relatively healthy place to live – clean water, good air at high altitude and the ability to drain away sewage and refuse down the natural slopes all contributed to less disease and longer lifespans than in many other towns and burghs. Furthermore, the agricultural lands of the Carse of Stirling were fertile and produced decent crops, despite the inefficient farming methods of the day, and this meant that there were few food shortages.

Expansion of industry had created the need for more institutions to handle monetary affairs and raise investment capital. By this time the financial system in Scotland had become more sophisticated. In 1695 the Bank of Scotland had been established (by an Englishman, the year after the Bank of England was established by a Scotsman) mainly to stimulate trade with England and the Low Countries and to issue notes as an alternative to the notoriously unreliable Scots coinage. However, it became increasingly associated with the Jacobite persuasion and in 1727 the Royal Bank of Scotland was created as a Hanoverian counterweight. The British Linen Bank, founded to foster the cloth industry, followed in 1746. The Stirling Bank Company was set up in 1777 with the Merchant Banking Company of Stirling coming later. The stage was set for the exploitation of Stirling's resources. It was at about this time the guilds were starting to lose their political grip on the burgh.

George Mouat, silk merchant, wearing the robes and symbols of office of the Dean of the Guildry. He was a member of the Guildry for almost seventy years, twice dean and died in 1893. The Guildry survived the dilution of its powers in the nineteenth century and exists today, essentially as a charitable body. (*BD*)

For the previous century or so the burgh council of Stirling consisted of twenty-one members – fourteen from the Guildry and seven from the trades. The inbuilt guild majority led to abuses and in particular enabled some to keep themselves and their friends continuously in office. This abuse was taken before the Court of Session and the Michaelmas 1773 election of magistrates and councillors was declared null and void. An appeal to the House of Lords failed and the burgh was effectively disenfranchised. This unhappy situation lasted for almost eight years until 1781 when George IV responded to a petition from the burgesses and townspeople, restoring the burgh but imposing poll elections for the magistracy and town council, ending the Guildry's stranglehold for ever.

The rules of entry to the Guildry maintained its selectiveness. From 1520 onwards admission required a payment of £5, with candlewax and wine, unless the applicant were the eldest son of a Guildry member. Later this condition was eased so a father could choose which son might be proposed for admission.

The Guildry ring, seen here depicted in a window of the Church of the Holy Rude. This ring of gold with a cross made of five jewels – amethyst, emerald, garnet, ruby and crystal – may have been a gift from David II in 1360. (Stirling Council)

Women were not admitted until well into the 1900s. By this time, though, the benefits of membership were less marked. The Burgh Trading Act of 1846 entitled anyone to open a shop or trade within the town and abolished the distinction between freemen of the town and 'unfreemen'. This reined in the Guildry and the trades and blunted their exclusive privileges, though the influence of both remains, largely in a ceremonial sense. In 1984 a Guildry Trust Fund was established to raise money for charitable and community projects, and has the Queen and Princess Anne among its honorary members. The Guildry still meets a few times a year. The Dean of the Guildry takes an oath annually, wearing the green and gold robes of office with a gold chain, dating from 1822, and a replica of the Guildry ring. The use of ecclesiastic titles for Guildry officials (dean, deacon, kirk-maister) derives from the importance of the medieval church and from the fact that the officials paid all the expenses of a special altar and services in the parish church.

At the end of the Jacobite era, Stirling no longer needed to be a defended town and developed into something resembling its present structure. As the burgh spread beyond its defensive but confining walls, the town gates disappeared. Elegant Georgian suburbs emerged under the influence of architect and builder Alexander Bowie and turnpikes replaced the old cart tracks and drove roads into the town. Eventually, the disenfranchisement of the burgh from 1773 to 1781 and the wider electoral reforms of 1833 removed their Guildry's ability to pack the council and the Free Trade Act of 1846 put an end to their commercial monopoly. Where the new industries established themselves was determined by the availability of raw materials and power sources, like water and coal.

Breweries, textile mills, distilleries, tanneries and paper making all relied on water. It was also the source of Stirling salmon, which was highly valued and sent in huge quantities to Glasgow and London. The River Forth would also prove important to Stirling as the Industrial Revolution progressed. The Forth–Clyde canal, opened in 1790, increased trade and the first truly practical steam paddle-boat, Symington's *Charlotte Dundas*, partly built at Carron, was demonstrated at Camelon in 1802. It pulled two 70-ton barges 20 miles along the canal in just 6 hours. However, the Falkirk authorities feared its wash would damage the canal banks and it was never used to its full potential. Nevertheless, the seed was planted and led to greater than ever river and canal traffic. Stirling's harbour at Shore Road had to be enlarged to deal with the increased business.

Coal Mining

The effects of the Industrial Revolution were mainly felt in the coal mining industry, concentrated south-east of Stirling. Again, this is a consequence of Stirling's geography. Central Scotland, from Fife in the east to Ayrshire in the west, sits on a belt of carboniferous coal deposits. These had been exploited by open-cast mining since early medieval times, usually by digging into a hillside. Mine shafts and bell pits were excavated, but not deep as miners had to scale up and down ladders. The English army bought coal in Stirlingshire

THE RADICAL REBELLION

The year 1820 saw two Stirling men hanged and beheaded for 'rebellion'. The spirit of the Declaration of Arbroath of exactly 500 years earlier had woven itself into the fabric of many societies. The American Revolution with its insistence on 'no taxation without representation'; the French Revolutionary principles of 'Liberty, Equality, Fraternity'; the inspirational writings of Robert Burns and Tom Paine and their insistence on the 'Rights of Man'; and the growth of literacy all combined to foment discussions about politics and social conditions among workers, and particularly weavers who worked mostly at home and were of an independent spirit, but organised. From 1790 the British government felt increasingly threatened. In 1793, a Unitarian minister, Thomas Fysshe Palmer, was sentenced to seven years' transportation for distributing political tracts and pamphlets. In 1798 George Mealmaker, a member of various subversive organisations with high-sounding names like 'The Friends of Liberty' and 'The United Scotsmen', was given fourteen years transportation for 'planning to establish a Republican Government'. In 1807 the Sutherland Clearances had taken place, a government policy under which Highlanders and their lifestyle were removed from 90 per cent of the Highlands to make way for sheep farming. And 1746 was still within living memory, when the wearing of the kilt, the display of tartan and clan gatherings were made punishable by death. Centuries-old Highland culture was effectively wiped out.

In 1812 a nine-week widespread weavers' strike spurred the authorities into setting up a network of informers. By 1817 unemployment was rising and wages falling, a situation exacerbated by the slump caused by the ending of hostilities with France in 1815, the demobilisation of 400,000 soldiers back to Britain and a wave of Irish emigration after the potato famine. Parliament passed various draconian measures, including a ban on mass meetings and suspension of habeas corpus to allow them to deal with the frightening tide of revolution. In August 1819 a peaceful reform meeting at St Peter's Field in Manchester was broken up by military force. Of the 80,000 present, largely weavers, 11 were killed and some 500 injured. This 'Peterloo massacre' provoked demonstrations all over Scotland, including rioting in Paisley which required the use of cavalry to restrain perhaps 5,000 'Radicals', as they became known.

By October, Gilbert McLeod's newsheet, *The Spirit of Union*, was being widely disseminated and a meeting in Stirling saw 2,000 people attend. Government informers and *agents provocateurs* discovered plans to establish a Scottish provisional government and identified the committee responsible – twenty-seven of them were arrested in February 1820. In a repeat of the tactics used to crush the Covenanters of the 1670s, the arrests were kept secret so that the supporters were tricked into open rebellion in the belief that they had won their liberty, then they were identified and dealt with. On Monday 3 April there were a series of strikes in support of a provisional government. This may have involved upwards of 50,000 throughout Scotland, including Stirlingshire. Deprived of their leadership, they stumbled into a poorly planned insurrection. A small, ill-organised band of weavers and other workers headed by John Baird and Andrew Hardie marched from Glasgow Green intending to seize the munitions at the Carron Iron Works in Falkirk. They were met by another group from Stirling. But they unwisely told their plans to a traveller who, along with a turncoat called King, alerted the Stirling Castle authorities and the army at Kilsyth. The thirty-odd men were ridden down in a brutal cavalry charge by sixteen Hussars supported by sixteen Yeomanry, known thereafter as the Battle of Bonnymuir. A number, including Baird and Hardie, were arrested and taken to Stirling Castle. A third group from Strathaven was dispersed.

In August 1820, one Radical leader, James Wilson, was hung and beheaded at Glasgow Green for his part in the Strathaven Rising, in front of a crowd of 20,000 sympathisers. (His last words, to his executioner, were: 'Did you ever see such a crowd, Thomas?') On 8 September 1820 Baird and Hardie were sentenced to be hung and beheaded at Stirling Tolbooth for leading the Radicals at Bonnymuir; the charge was high treason. Nineteen others were sentenced to be hung, but sensing the public mood and juries' unwillingness to convict, the authorities commuted the sentences to transportation to New South Wales and shied away from other mass arrests. Hardie himself, on the scaffold, urged the crowd to go home and read their Bibles rather than provoke any further unrest – a speech that had exactly the opposite effect. Feelings ran so high that the two opposing lawyers, Hullock and Jeffray, almost had a duel after the trial. They later made up and became friends. Working-class consciousness had arrived, to match the middle classes new-found identity. But thereafter it found expression in a moral force and Chartism rather than physical violence and open rebellion. Whig politics ousted the Duke of Wellington's government and the Reform Acts widened the electoral franchise from fewer than 1 per cent of men before 1832 to about 1 in over 8 afterwards.

It would be good to be able to report that this affluence spread to the general populace, but most often men, women and children worked for long hours in poor conditions, for low pay and living in overcrowded housing. For instance, by 1841 the nail-making village of St Ninians, just south of Stirling, employed a high proportion of children, many of whom worked 6 days a week, making over 1,000 nails in a 16-hour day for not much more than a shilling. A similar situation obtained at Camelon, where Caddell of Carronpark brought workmen from England to teach the trade to the locals. By 1830 he had over 500 nail makers employed. A man working five or six 10-hour days could earn up to 14s (70p) a week; but machine-made nails from the USA and London ruined the hand-made trade.

during the Scottish Wars of Independence, probably so their blacksmiths could forge and repair weapons. There were at least two coal mines in Stirling in the mid-sixteenth century, but most people used peat and wood for cooking and to heat their homes. However, both became depleted by overuse and by 1800 a substantial coal industry had started at Plean and Bannockburn. Also, the Industrial Revolution created an almost insatiable demand for the 'black diamonds' and deep mining on a commercial scale became economically viable. By 1783, there were seventeen pits in operation at Bannockburn. As the industry expanded and families left their home villages to find work in the new mines, whole new communities like Cowie, Fallin and Plean were created around the pit heads to provide them with housing.

Coal was the key to the Industrial Revolution. It fired the boilers that made steam to power the looms of machine production. It smelted the iron and steel to make the looms and the railway lines and trains that carried finished goods to the customers. And it powered the trains themselves. Also, it fuelled the manufacture of the vast supplies needed while Britain pursued various overseas wars from 1793 until 1815.

Nothing worked without coal. And no coal could be got without miners. From 1597 any vagrant could be branded and claimed as a slave. Even 200 years later, Scottish miners were bonded by law to their mines. A miner could not leave a mine and if the mine were sold, the bondsmen were sold with it. Miners tolerated this because they were paid slightly higher wages, but they were little more than feudal serfs. This was not abolished until the passing of the Thirlage Act in 1799. One of the paradoxes of the Industrial Revolution was that while its effect was to mechanise most industries, the coal on which it was based was still dug out with picks and shovels and hauled to the surface in hutches by pit ponies. Until outlawed by Parliament in 1842, women and children worked below the surface alongside their husbands and fathers. The children were small enough to work in spaces too cramped for adults. Working on their knees and crawling along dark, dank tunnels on their bellies, miners were at risk from roof collapses and explosions as their gas or tallow lamps sparked fire damp. As late as 1922 an explosion at Plean killed twelve miners and devastated the small community.

Up until the early 1900s women were employed at the pit head as 'pickers' – meeting the coal as it came up from the pit, picking out any stones and breaking up larger lumps of coal with heavy hammers before loading it onto wagons. At about this time new mines opened and workers came from all over Britain to work and live in the Stirling area. The pressure on housing

Also known as St Ringans, the ancient village of St Ninians is a mile south of Stirling centre and is now part of the city. In the eighteenth and nineteenth centuries it was a coal-mining, nail-making and tartan-weaving centre. The prominent tower of the parish church dates from 1734 and is the only part of the kirk to have survived an explosion in 1745 when it was used by the Jacobites as an arsenal. The church was rebuilt in 1751 on a separate site. Some of the seventeenth and eighteenth century building in Kirk Wynd still stand. (*Stirling Council*)

was great and many found cheap accommodation in Stirling, often miles from their pits. The old town landlords subdivided existing buildings into tiny one- and two-room flats. In 1908 the average population density for the burgh was 14 people per acre – there were 290 per acre living in Broad Street. Gradually the mining companies realised it was in their interests to provide decent housing close to the mines for their workers. The accommodation blocks they built were basic by today's standards, but better than the tenement slums in Stirling's old town. A family would have one room with a sink and fireplace with a smaller bedroom off – many a young couple started their married life in this small room at the house of a parent or relative until other accommodation became available for them. Toilets were shared, cooking was over an open fire and in a recess that served as an oven and lighting was by paraffin lamps. Laundry was done in a communal wash-house or 'steamie', which also acted as a community centre, the wives and older daughters socialising as they scrubbed the clothes and hung them out on the green to dry.

The First World War changed everything. Men left the mines to fight and came back resolved to improve their situations. Women discovered new strengths and capabilities. The mines experienced a short boom during the worldwide fuel crisis, but in 1921 prices slumped. Mine owners cut wages and reduced output, which meant sacking miners, who responded with two strikes in 1921 and 1926. In Stirling, the industrial action was peaceful and short-lived, but cheap foreign imports and competition from oil, as well as the Depression, meant that by 1932, a third of British miners were out of work. Even nationalisation in 1947 could not halt the decline. Mines everywhere started to close. One Stirling pit stayed open – Polmaise, near Fallin – but it was the announcement of its closure that provoked the 1984 miners' strike across all Britain. Polmaise closed in July 1987 and a centuries-old tradition died. Scotland's very last deep mine at nearby Longannet closed in 2002 after a disastrous flood.

Textiles

Other industries developed and grew during the Industrial Revolution. Stagecoaches had improved Stirling's communications and trade links with the rest of Scotland. Stirling became a significant wool-making town, the mills powered by local streams. Bannockburn was famous for tartan weaving, at one time making about 90 per cent of the world's tartan in mills established in the 1770s. The origin of this cloth is unknown. It is usually thought of as a Highland Gaelic phenomenon, but its origin may pre-date the arrival of the Irish Scots in the fourth and fifth centuries. William Wilson & Sons of Bannockburn were the first industrial producers of tartan. They started their industrial production of it at a time when the wearing of tartan was prohibited by law in the aftermath of the Jacobite rebellions. Paradoxically, the prohibition created an interest in tartan beyond the Highlands and at its repeal the cloth became fashionable. Wilson's were also the earliest known recorders of tartan manufacture – their Key Pattern Book of 1819 documents the instructions for more than 200 tartan designs produced at their Bannockburn weaving sheds and dye works. The same year

Originally a Bronze Age settlement and later a Roman camp, Cambusbarron is an ancient village to the south-east of Stirling, now separated from it by the M80 motorway. A former spinning and woollen manufacturing settlement, with weaving done in cottages like those above, it was home to Parkvale and Hayford mills, which employed more than a thousand workers. Hayford (below) was founded by the Smiths in 1833, later became a barracks, sat unused for fifteen years and is now a residential development. (*SCLS*)

George, Prince of Wales gave Stirling cloth a great boost by having a Highland outfit made which he wore with great pride during his visit in 1822. Wilson's continued to produce tartan at Bannockburn until 1840. This growth in textile manufacture also spawned the Hayford Mills at Cambusbarron and Pullars' Dye Works at Bridge of Allan.

Another spur to diversification in the textile industry was the wars of 1793 to 1815 which had caused a recession in the export-driven wool and cloth markets, mainly due to the blockage of the main trading port of Brugge. But other manufactures took their place. Stirling cotton was highly prized within Britain and carpet weaving started. MacGregor's factory was a major employer (along with Stevenson's wool mill), both making use of the stream that ran from the castle rock to Port Street and employing the factory system, which was gradually replacing the home-weaving cottage industry.

New Industry

The coming of the railway to Stirling in the 1840s changed the burgh more radically than at any time before or since. New Victorian suburbs sprang up to house commuters from Glasgow and on the back of this new shops, business premises and amenities were established to service their needs. A number of excellent and distinctive buildings date from the nineteenth century, all functional and all in keeping with the overall look and feel of the town. Among the best are the Albert Halls, the Stirling Smith Art Gallery and Museum and the many architectural works of Bowie, as well as the commercial buildings at the Alhambra and the Arcade.

The cumulative effects of the repeal of the anti-organised labour Combination Laws and the Corn Laws and the introduction of the electoral reforms in the 1830s and the Burgh Trading Act of 1846 saw a great expansion in the number and nature of independent businesses serving the town and the surrounding area. Foundries, chemical factories and rope works opened alongside coopering, brickmaking, calico printing, paper making, quarrying and the expected brewing and distilling businesses, as well as more woollen mills and dye works.

Nearby at Campsie a certain Charles Macintosh was busy trying to find a use for the waste products of gasworks and discovered that coal-tar naphtha could dissolve rubber and adhere it to cloth, thereby developing the waterproofing technology that still bears his name. Pottery also started at about this time. The Dunmore estate near Airth began making bricks and tiles for building repairs, but also produced domestic cookware using clay from the Carse of Stirling. The diggings unearthed 8,000-year-old whale bones, presumably washed there by a tidal wave. From 1835 to 1902, under the control of third-generation potter Peter Gardner, Dunmore pottery became fashionable and is still sought after today.

Silver was for a while a major commodity. The Alva silver mine on the edge of the Ochil Hills, now barren, was part of the richest silver deposit in Britain. It was the source of Stirling (sterling) silver, now defined as 925 fine (925 parts silver and 75 parts copper) and is the origin of the Pound Sterling.

Stirling silver was highly prized not only for currency but also for artifacts, like these communion cups. (*Stirling Smith Art Gallery and Museum*)

Transport

The retail trade had begun in earnest in the mid-1800s. And since these new consumers required transport, coachbuilding thrived. Carriages had first been seen in Stirling during the sixteenth century, but only for the wealthy. Now they were more commonly used, with even tourists travelling in them. A mail coach service had run between Edinburgh and Perth since 1784 and as Stirling was more or less halfway between them, it was the perfect place to carry out any repairs made necessary by the rough roads. From 1792 the Stirling Light Coach Company ran a daily passenger service to Edinburgh, fare 8s 6d (43p), starting from the Saracen's Head, an inn at the corner of Friars Street and King Street, now the site of a bank.

In 1802 William Croall and his ex-apprentice, Henry Kinross, opened premises in Shore Road, moving in about 1865 to Port Street in the building now occupied by Marks & Spencer. Their customers were definitely upmarket – in 1816 Sir David Baird, fresh from campaigning with the Duke of Wellington in the Peninsular Wars, commissioned a family carriage. The peak of the company's success came in 1837 when Henry Kinross received the royal warrant as coach maker to Queen Victoria. When Victoria visited Stirling in 1842, Kinross built a special seventy-seater coach to ride behind her cavalcade. They also made coaches for the Scottish Central Railway. In 1850 a fire destroyed the Kinross works, but the company somehow built an 'improved' street omnibus which was on display at the Great Exhibition the following year, winning a silver medal. This gained them new customers from India, South Africa, the Caribbean and elsewhere. For years the luxurious and brightly painted phaetons built for the Indian market were a mainstay of the business. By 1910 they felt justified in advertising themselves as 'Carriage and Motor Car builders to the Nobility and Gentry of Great Britain, His Highness the Rajah of Jowar and many other Native Gentlemen of India'. Croall's sons left the company and Henry Kinross had no son of his own, so the business passed to his nephew William. William Kinross & Sons claimed to have made the first 'gig' – a light two-wheeled hoodless carriage – in Scotland.

Retail

Stirling was still a seat of government, albeit as a county town rather than a royal residence. So it naturally became the market centre with a wide variety of shops and services providing for the surrounding area – not only the mundane butchers, grocers and dairies could be found there, but photographers, dressmakers, milliners, hairdressers and the professions such as lawyers, doctors and architects.

Crawford's Arcade, opened in 1882, was a retail innovation – a covered street. (*NP*)

THE STIRLING JUG

Scotland will doubtless one day give up the inch, foot, yard and mile in favour of the more logical metric system, just as it previously dropped the Pound Scots, the ell, the reel, the boll, the chopin, the firlot and the farthing. But the pint is another, altogether more emotive measurement. The Stirling Jug is said to have been established in 1457 by the burgh council to regulate liquid measures but is mentioned in acts of Parliament as being in the town before the reign of James II in 1437. It was the yardstick by which all other Scottish quantities were standardised and was not superseded until Imperial measures were introduced in 1707. By an act of the Scottish Parliament, Edinburgh kept the standard ell, Lanark the pound, Linlithgow the firlot, Perth the reel and Stirling the pint jug, an arrangement intended to improve commerce by checking frauds and because each of the commodities to which these different standards applied were predominantly supplied by the respective towns in whose care they were placed. Clearly, Edinburgh was then the principal market for cloth (hence its Lawnmarket), Lanark for wool, Linlithgow for grain, Perth for yarn and we can infer that Stirling had the monopoly on beers, wines and spirits. The last mention of the jug is in an Act of Parliament of 19 February 1618, in the reign of James VI. No accurate

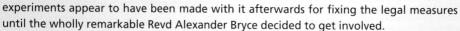

experiments appear to have been made with it afterwards for fixing the legal measures until the wholly remarkable Revd Alexander Bryce decided to get involved.

In 1750 Bryce, minister of Kirknewton and already well known as a geometrician, visited Stirling. Given his interest in mensuration and knowing that the burgh had the responsibility of keeping the pint jug as the standard for liquid and dry measure in Scotland, he asked the magistrates if he could see it. He was referred to the council chambers where a pewter pint jug was kept suspended from the ceiling. Bryce examined it in minute detail and announced that it could not be the actual standard. The magistrates were less than bothered but Bryce, being both an antiquary and a mathematician, decided to recover the original. His search for this valuable antique over the next two years was in vain. But in 1752 it occurred to him that the jug might have been borrowed by a brazier or coppersmith, in order to make accurate replicas. Discovering that a craftsman called Urquhart had joined the rebel forces in 1745 never to return and that his furniture and utensils had been sold at public auction, Bryce tracked down an attic where unsold articles had been discarded as useless. To no one's surprise greater than his own, Bryce found the object of his search under a load of lumber. The embarrassment of its supposed guardians at this early 'Antiques Road Show' must have been acute.

They could then hardly deny Revd Bryce's request to take the jug to Edinburgh, the better to measure it precisely with an accurate spirit level and scales. After seventeen trials with 'clear Leith water', some in the presence of Edinburgh magistrates, the jug was found to hold 54 ounces, 8 drops and 20 grains (26,180 grains English troy weight), and its volume to be 103.404 cubic inches. From this standard Scots pint, Bryce determined the chopin to be 51.702 cubic inches and the mutchkin 25.851 cubic inches. Mathematicians will have spotted that the Scots pint is almost exactly three English pints and equals two chopins or four mutchkins.

The actual Stirling Jug. It is a hollow brass truncated cone 4.17 inches across at the mouth and 5.25 inches at the base, 6 inches deep, with a handle. On the front are a shield and lion rampant of Scotland and near the bottom is another shield. Below this is the letter S, presumably intended to indicate Stirling, as well as an animal that could either be a wolf (which would make sense) or, as some claim, an ape (which would make no sense at all). (*Stirling Smith Art Gallery and Museum*)

Similarly, Bryce worked out the legal measures for grain – the wheat and pease firlot were 21¼ Stirling pints and the bear (barley) and oat firlot 31 pints, which allowed him to define the peck, the lippie and the boll and compare them to the English bushel. To quote Bryce: 'A Scotch barley boll contains 5 bushels, 3 pecks, 2 lippies, and a little more, according to the Winchester gallon' and 'A Scotch chalder (16 bolls of barley) is equal to 11 quarters, 6 bushels, and 3 lippies, Winchester measure'. And since, by an Act of Parliament in 1618, the Scots pint contains 'of the clear running water of Leith three pounds and seven ounces, French troy weight'; therefore in the Scots pound there are '7616 troy grains; and in the Scotch ounce 476 troy grains'. Bryce clearly took it all very seriously. He was then invited to see to the adjustment of the weights and measures kept by the Dean of the Guildry; and 'for his good services to the city' was made a burgess and guild brother in January 1754.

Beyond his attachment to the accuracy of Scots measurement, Bryce also published accounts of a new comet (1766), observations on the transits of Venus in 1761 and 1769, a novel method of measuring the velocity of the wind, the use of the barometer for measuring altitudes and the water equivalent of snowfall. In 1767 he was consulted on the surveys for the Forth and Clyde Canal and helped plan Mackenzie's observatory at Belmont Castle. All of this led to his appointment in 1774 by the magistrates of Stirling to consult on the supply of water to the burgh, which involved measuring levels, calculating the correct sizes for lead pipes and the reservoir and suggesting where it should be placed. He later received the freedom of the burgh. An excellent lecturer as well as a renowned preacher, Bryce sadly left no notes or sermons for publication, although several songs and poetry, mainly devotional, do remain. He also became a close friend of James Douglas, 14th Earl of Morton (1702–68) and was the first president of what became the Royal Society of Edinburgh. Bryce's final triumph, a few days before his death in 1786, was to confirm Sir Isaac Newton's prediction of the relationship between the earth's axis and its diameter as 221:222.

The growth of a well-off middle class brought changes to the way people bought and sold their goods – instead of going to markets and craft workshops, they began to use shops. These establishments, no longer restricted to trading locally, bought goods from a wide range of suppliers, offering a greater choice and adding their own profit to the price. It would probably be fair to say that tourism, with the associated retail, transport and distributive jobs, remains Stirling's main industry. But retail has steadily become more and more prominent. Until the mid-1600s goods and provisions were bought and sold either from market stalls or 'foreshops' – booths built on the fronts of buildings. Bread and vegetables were sold at the Mercat Cross; the butter and poultry market was in St John Street; the meal market in Spittal Street sold seeds and grain; and the meat market stood at the head of Back Walk. This was still the pattern until the early 1800s. While markets still existed and were an important sector of the economy, shops as we know them started to emerge. There were three main stimuli to this – the arrival of affordable plate glass, and therefore shop window displays; improved transport by rail and road which expanded the range of goods available; and increased demand from a public with tastes that were growing steadily more sophisticated. The influx of commuters, used to the shops of Glasgow and Edinburgh, must have played a large part. The first new grocery businesses to open were D. & J. MacEwan in Broad Street (1807) and Cowborough & McNab in Port Street (1839). The meal market was pulled down in 1814 and replaced by the Athenaeum, or The Steeple, with two shops on the ground floor, as today. Menzies the draper and milliner made the best use of large glass windows with a modern shop opened in 1864. Markets and fairs for livestock and horses continued into the 1870s but the transition to shops much like those of today was completed with the opening of the Crawford Arcade in 1882, a fashionable shopping gallery sheltered from the weather.

The retail emporia of the nineteenth century still dominate many townscapes, and deservedly so. Stirling's arcade was privately financed by William Crawford, a councillor, on lands he had cannily acquired over the years. The theatre at its heart was dubbed the 'Town Hall', somewhat inappropriately. The Murray Place end had the former Arcade Hotel and the King Street access was described as 'Tuileries-style' by its designer John McLean. It shows another aspect of Stirling's daring to be different, in that while privately owned and managed by the Arcade Association of retailers who occupied it, the lighting was provided by the council and it was effectively a public street. The builders couldn't have foreseen tanning parlours, electronic games shops and fast-food restaurants, but the original atmosphere has been retained.

Looking forward

In 1900 electricity arrived in Stirling and other new technologies spawned novel industries, among them the Stirling Gas Light Company, the Grampian Motor Company and Alexander's Buses. And, of course, there was aviation under the Barnwell brothers. Stirling survived two world wars more or less undamaged in physical terms but at great human cost and the twentieth century saw the town council tackle deprivation and slum housing, poverty and unemployment in the 1930s, urban regeneration in the 1940s and 1950s and the arrival of new industries from the 1960s onwards. The burgh emerged as a fully fledged city at the start of the new millennium. But before considering the twentieth century, it is important to look at the development of tourism, such an important part of Stirling's past and present, in the century before.

6

A Most Desirable Destination

The Napoleonic Wars of the early nineteenth century provided an unpredicted benefit to Stirling and the surrounding area. Writers and artists of the century before had undertaken Grand Tours in Europe, but this was not now possible. Instead, they came north, attracted by grandeur and beauty that clearly beat the Lake District hands down.

At about the same time, Sir Walter Scott was bankrupt and decided the only way to raise money was to write best-sellers. He found much of his inspiration in Scotland's history, characters and landscape – most notably his epic poem *The Lady of the Lake* (1810), *Waverley* (1814) and the somewhat fanciful retelling of the story of *Rob Roy* (1817). These put Stirlingshire, Loch Katrine and the Trossachs on the map and prompted an upsurge in tourism.

Waverley, Scott's first published novel, particularly thumped the tub of Gaelic romanticism, as an aristocratic young army officer is posted to Scotland during the 1745 Jacobite rebellion and finds much to admire in the vitality of the traditional culture, especially the poetry and music. He describes the anarchic and feudalistic clan system, the honour and bravery of the warrior clansmen and the juxtaposition between the barbaric aspects of Highland life and the sophistication of many of the inhabitants – the heroine, Flora, had studied in Paris and played the harp. The existence of an unknown 'noble savage' culture right on the doorstep induced many English (and even Lowland Scots, who knew little of their neighbours further north) to go and see it first hand.

Scott is also justifiably credited with the invention of clan tartans. In 1818 he had rediscovered the Honours of Scotland (crown, sword and sceptre) walled up in Edinburgh Castle and in 1822 was presented with an unmissable opportunity to show off the splendour of Scotland's past and present, when King George IV visited. George, recently freed from the burden of his deaf, blind and mad father who died in 1820 and from his uncrowned and detested queen, Caroline of Brunswick who had obligingly passed away the next year, was feeling his oats and flexing his new-found royal muscles. The visit, the first by a British monarch to Scotland since 1650, was also what we would call today a PR stunt, a response to the Radical Rebellions

Images like this early postcard of Stirling Castle were an outcome and a standard depiction of tourism in the nineteenth and early twentieth centuries. (*BD*)

Opposite: Sir Walter Scott, whose romantic poems, novels and ballads stimulated the early tourist trade. (*BD*)

SCOTLAND'S CHAUCER

Perhaps the earliest exhortation to visit Stirling for its summer pleasures, rather than to conquer its castle, comes from Sir David Lindsay, often called 'Scotland's Chaucer'. In his 1538 *Testament and Complaynt of Our Soverane Lordis Papyngo* (popinjay, or parrot), he puts into the mouth of the king's dying pet bird the regret that it will miss Snowdon (an ancient name for Stirling). Really, it was a satire on the hypocrisy and greed of certain birds of prey – in other words, the clergy – and was a cornerstone of the Reformation.

Adew, fair Snawdown! With thy touris hie
Thy Chapell Royall, park and tabyll rounde!
May, June and July walde I dwell in thee
War I ane man, to heir the birdies sounde
Quhilk doith agane thy royall roche redounde.

Robert Burns, an eighteenth-century tourist to Stirling, had similar views about the loss of Stirling's glory during the Hanoverian times.

and mass popular uprisings of 1819–22. Scott, placed in charge of arrangements for the royal visit, conceived the idea of asking the main clan chiefs to attend His Majesty dressed 'in the masquerade of the Celtic Society'. Before this, the clan system – in existence for a relatively short time – had existed to provide fighting troops who were distinguished from each other by wearing a cockade, a sprig of heather or some other plant in their bonnets. Tartans, if they denoted anything, would have been indicative of a locality rather than a family or clan affiliation. But the clan chiefs, and the populace in general, took to the idea of tartans and the whole country went crazy for plaids and pipes. The king himself wore a kilt, woven in Bannockburn, although he rather spoiled the effect by wearing it over a pair of incongruous pink tights. Not everyone was quite so wholehearted about the tartan commotion. Walter Scott's son-in-law, J.G. Lockhart, later referred to the visit of George IV as a 'collective hallucination', in which Scotland was identified with the Highlanders, 'a small, almost insignificant part of the Scottish people'.

Nonetheless, the tartan industry was firmly established and became even more solidly implanted during the Victorian era. It continues to be the major defining element of Scottishness worldwide – a simple, colourful, impressionistic 'brand image' for Scotland which, most importantly, worked. Later tourist boards could learn much from this.

The natural result was that more and more people wanted to visit the north. Travel was becoming easier with improved roads and coach services to Stirling from Edinburgh and Glasgow and from Stirling to Alloa, Callander

Stirling was not slow to capitalise on the popularity of Walter Scott's novels, as witness the Waverley Temperance Hotel near the north parish church in Murray Place, seen here in this early lithograph. (*SCLS*)

W.Y. MACGREGOR

Typical of artists who took inspiration from the area around Stirling was William York MacGregor, 1855–1923. Known as W.Y., he was the 'father of the Glasgow Boys', an influential group of painters in the late nineteenth and early twentieth centuries. He was the son of John MacGregor, partner in the shipbuilding firm of Tod & MacGregor, who died when W.Y. was less than three years old, leaving him financially independent. After schooldays at Western Academy in Glasgow he and his friend James Paterson went on to the Glasgow School of Art and painted together from 1877 at St Andrews, Stonehaven and Nairn, practising the new form of plein-air painting.

The Glasgow Art Club rejected them as members so they left the city, W.Y. to train at the Slade in London under Alphonse Legros. Later, W.Y. returned to Glasgow and started the studio at 134 Bath Street which became the meeting place for Crawhall, Walton, Henry, Lavery, his friend James Paterson and others who became known as the 'Glasgow Boys'. W.Y.'s 1884 picture, the *Vegetable Stall* (in Edinburgh's National Gallery), is one of the most important realist paintings produced in Scotland. His 1883 work *Crail* is in the Stirling Smith Art Gallery and Museum.

W.Y. suffered from asthma and moved to Allen Bank, Bridge of Allan, to convalesce. He also spent time in Worthing and in South Africa. His health improved but homesickness prompted a return to Bridge of Allan. In 1898 he was elected to the Royal Scottish Academy. Fond of food, cigars and reading, he drank little and was always shy with women. By 1901 he was living at Albyn Lodge, Bridge of Allan with his mother and half-sister. He finally married in 1923 aged sixty-eight but died five months later.

RELIABLE SERIES No. 142/6

Logie Old Church, the last resting place of William York MacGregor (1855–1923), 'father of the Glasgow Boys', his wife Jessie Watson and his half-sister Jenny. (*Stirling Council*)

and Perth. A Scotsman living in New York had returned home and invented the road-surfacing process which still bears his name – MacAdam.

Coach trips also took visitors to the fashionable spa at Bridge of Allan, which started to be developed in the 1820s. Robert Louis Stevenson, possibly inspired by his visits to Bridge of Allan to take the waters in 1859, 1865, 1872 and 1875, and the fact that his grandfather had built the bridge nearby, set his novels *Kidnapped* and *Catriona* in the Stirlingshire countryside. Artists were drawn there to seek out the settings of these literary works and capture them on canvas. By Stevenson's time a number of famous artists had settled in and around Stirling, notably Joseph Denovan Adam, William Kennedy, one of the 'Glasgow Boys', at Cambuskenneth and later W.Y. MacGregor at Bridge of Allan. Many others came to find inspiration for landscapes and pastoral works.

Queen Victoria's passion for Scotland did much to increase the attraction of the Stirling area for others. Tourism began to organise itself and to cater for different markets and pockets, and over 100 years ago the SS *Sir Walter Scott* started to ply its pleasure trade along Loch Katrine.

Bridge of Allan

If ever there was a community purposefully developed to capitalise on tourism, it is Bridge of Allan. Not 3 miles from the centre of Stirling, it is the classic Victorian boom town, but has retained most of its village charm.

Before the railways – and to a lesser extent after – the horse and carriage provided the means to get around Stirling and its surroundings. Archibald Campbell opened the Royal Hotel in 1840 and also ran coach services to and from Glasgow, Callander and elsewhere. Sharp as a pin, Campbell offered cheap fares to those wishing to take the waters at the newly fashionable spa of Bridge of Allan and did not miss the trick of giving his coaches names from Scott's popular romances, such as 'Rob Roy', and 'Lady of the Lake'. (*SCLS*)

Situated by the Allan Water and overlooked by the Wallace Monument and the Ochil Hills, the elegant Victorian buildings are a testimony to its growth as a tourism and health centre in the nineteenth century. The clachan of Bridgend was the community that grew into Bridge of Allan, and the earliest record of a bridge is 1520.

The Ochils provided both copper – mined at the nearby settlement of Pathfoot in the sixteenth century and sporadically up to 1815 – and an excellent water supply water. In the 1820s, Sir Robert Abercromby of the neighbouring Airthrey estate (now home to the University of Stirling) was well aware of the growing fashion for health spas and the difficulties of visiting European watering places. He had also spotted the potential in the growing numbers of visitors to the area, drawn by the writings of Sir Walter Scott, whose *The Lady of the Lake* written a decade before was bringing visitors to the Trossachs in their droves.

Abercromby had the local waters analysed and, unsurprisingly, found they had curative properties. He built a well house in 1821 (long gone) and a spa pump room, now Kipling's Restaurant, in Mine Road. By 1836 Tait's *Edinburgh Magazine* had reported Bridge of Allan to be 'a delightful summer weekend retreat'. In 1844 the energetic Major Henderson inherited the Westerton estate and built much of the fine public and private architecture in the village, including purpose-built guest houses for those taking the waters. In 1848 the railway arrived, prompting further development including a bowling green, reading room and library.

This postcard dates from the early 1900s and shows the Allan Water Bridge. (*SCLS*)

The Allan Water Hotel, one of the well-known hydropathic resorts that were purpose-built in Bridge of Allan. (*SCLS*)

Henderson Street and the Royal Hotel, Bridge of Allan. (*BD*)

However, it was the publication of Dr Charles Rogers's 1851 pamphlet 'A Week at Bridge of Allan' which put the Airthrey wells and the township on the map. Over the next 25 years it swelled from a hamlet of some 300 souls to a town of ten times that number. The Victorian visitors attended the wells in the mornings, drinking three or four pints of the waters, then spent the rest of the day on walks, driving in the countryside, fishing and other pursuits. Bridge of Allan's main thoroughfare, Henderson Street, is a reminder of Major Henderson's sterling efforts in turning the village into a fashionable resort. It also boasts a number of interesting testimonials to his bravura style, notably the Fountain of Nineveh in Fountain Road, an 1852 folly with a cast-iron Doric column, erected to commemorate the excavations of the site of Nineveh on the River Tigris and to 'enhance the elegance of the town', as the plaque says. A heron was added to the top in 1895.

The Darn Walk riverside pathway is said to have been in use in Roman times and the 3-mile walk to Dunblane is associated with Robert Louis Stevenson, who included it in his adventure novel *Kidnapped*. A small cave by the river bank is possibly the inspiration for Ben Gunn's cave in *Treasure Island*. Charles Dickens was also among the many writers who visited Bridge of Allan during its heyday. (*Stirling Council*)

The National Wallace Monument

The creation of a national monument to William Wallace was first discussed in the early 1800s. This idea came on the back of a flood-tide of nationalism the whole world over and no less in Scotland. America and France had recently had revolutions. In 1818 Sir Walter Scott had rediscovered the crown, sword and sceptre of Scotland bricked up in Edinburgh Castle ever since the Union of Crowns in 1707 and his novels had fostered a re-awakening of interest in Scotland's history which had also created the tourism business. The Radical

THE RENNIE MACKINTOSH CONNECTION

It is quite incredible how many people – including art and architectural historians, do not know that Bridge of Allan's 1858 Holy Trinity Church has furnishings added by the famous Scots architect Charles Rennie Mackintosh in 1904. Two ladies of the congregation had left almost £900 for a new organ so the minister, the Revd Duncan Cameron, consulted his parishioner John Honeyman on a general refit. He was a partner in Keppie & Honeyman, the Glasgow firm who had just promoted a promising young apprentice, Mackintosh, to a partnership. His designs for the communion table and chair, the chancel rail, altar screen and pulpit were put into effect by John Craig, one of Mackintosh's favoured craftsman joiners. Mackintosh reduced his fee from £25 to £20 to save the church money. There were originally choir pews with ends carved to his designs, but these have since been removed and lost. Sadly, the significance of this was little realised and later some of the furnishings were mislaid. It was the Revd John Nicol who recognised their importance and drew attention to them. Now the Holy Trinity furnishings have an honoured place in the canon of Mackintosh's work. Another minister of Holy Trinity, the Revd Dr George Hendry, was instrumental in suggesting in 1946 the publication of a bible in the vernacular. This culminated in the production of the New English Bible in 1961.

The Rennie Mackintosh furnishings at Holy Trinity Church, Bridge of Allan. (*NP*)

O tempora, O mores! The Memorial Hall, once the museum, is fast becoming a 'residential development opportunity' and will doubtless find an appropriate use. (*SCLS*)

Rebellions of 1790 and 1820 and the subsequent Reform Acts of 1832 had shown the enthusiasm for Scottish secession and a wider political franchise. The outlawing of kilts and tartan in 1746 was still within living memory, and the memory stung. There were a number of revolutions in Europe in 1848 and Italian nationalism was leading inevitably towards Unification in 1860. Similarly, the German states were united in 1871.

Scottish nationalism was evident in 1853 with the establishment of the National Association for the Vindication of Scottish Rights. A national Wallace monument was a natural expression of Scotland's feelings at the time, and a committee of the great and good was convened in the 1830s. However, it took twenty years for any progress to be made. Initially, Edinburgh was the suggested site and as Scotland's capital, naturally expected to get it. Predictably Glasgow disagreed, and put forward plans for an erection on Glasgow Green, on the imaginative grounds that it already had the first monument to Lord Nelson (1806). Neither city had any real claim to Wallace. Other Scottish towns with a Wallace connection offered, but on the suggestion of the Revd Dr Charles Rogers, chaplain at Stirling Castle, it was agreed that Abbey Craig was the obvious and proper home for the National Wallace Monument. The land was available, as it had been owned by the Patrons of Cowane's Hospital since 1709.

The final decision was taken at a large meeting in the King's Park in 1856, and Edinburgh architect John T. Rochead's design for a Gothic tower overlooking the site of Wallace's 1297 victory at Stirling Bridge was the chosen option. Among many other nationalists from other countries, Garibaldi, 'the Wallace of Italy', sent a letter of support and announced his plans to visit. The Revd Dr Rogers became secretary in charge of raising funds, and by 1859 public donations from home and abroad had totalled almost £3,500. The foundation stone was laid on Bannockburn Day, 23 June 1861. A crowd of 50,000 to 70,000 were present (accounts vary, but the impact on Stirling's then population of 100,000 must have been considerable) with at least five bands playing 'Scots Wha' Hae', not necessarily in unison. But disputes among the National Monument Committee members and financial problems resulted in construction not being completed until 1869. In particular, the Revd Dr Rogers had been accused of excessive zeal in submitting his expenses and in 1863 he resigned his chaplaincy and left for London. Eventually public subscription collected £10,000 not only in Scotland but from Scots worldwide. This also inspired the erection of Wallace statues elsewhere, such as Baltimore in the USA and Ballarat in the Australian goldmining area.

The monument was handed over to the custodians and Stirling Town Council on 11 September 1869 – the 572nd anniversary of Wallace's victory – in a ceremony lasting only 30 minutes. Rogers stayed away, but his wife was presented with a portrait.

The 220-foot high Wallace Monument sits prominently on the Abbey Craig 2 miles north of Stirling. From this outstanding position Wallace watched the English army file across Stirling Bridge before leading the Scots into battle. It had acquired some new features in its 130-year history. Visitors walk from the foot of Abbey Craig (or take a minibus) and then ascend 246 steps through the monument's four levels. Level 1 (71 steps up) has a display on the life of Wallace and the Battle of Stirling Bridge, with a 3-D simulation of Wallace's own description of his trial at Westminster. The 700-year-old Wallace sword, almost 6 feet in length, over 2 inches wide at the guard and weighing 6 pounds, looks impossible to lift let alone fight with. And of course Wallace never did fight with it – despite claims by the Revd Dr Rogers that 'this great blade' had been taken from Wallace's pillow on the night of his capture at Robroyston in August 1305, we now know it to be a fake dating from the late sixteenth century. Despite earlier leaving Stirling under something of a cloud, Rogers returned in 1888 to oversee the handing over of the Wallace sword by Colonel Nightingale, commander of the garrison at Stirling Castle. He even managed to draw a comparison between himself and Wallace's uncle and tutor, Roger, also a priest.

The monument has seen its share of controversies since the financial and political shenanigans of the early days. On two occasions the Wallace sword – a fake but nonetheless a powerful symbol – has been stolen, once in 1836 and again in 1972. And it was at the centre of Stirling Council's 1995 decision – in the wake of a £1 million refurbishment of the tower – to abandon temporarily the bureaucratic-sounding 'Central Region' in favour of the less prosaic 'Braveheart County'. Most recently, the Abbey Craig has been found to be the site of a Pictish citadel dating from the Dark Ages, which will force a reappraisal of Stirling's importance as a tribal capital in the sixth to eighth centuries and makes the choice of the location for the monument even more apposite.

Level 2 (up 64 more steps) contains the Hall of Heroes, with marble statues of notable Scots, installed after a second worldwide appeal by the custodians in 1885. An audio-visual display is a twentieth-century addition. Level 3 (62 steps further up) has the Diorama, an illustration of the geography, important landmarks and historical battlefields surrounding the monument. Level 4 (at the top of the final 49 stairs) is 'The Crown' with its magnificent views all around. This is possibly the best vantage point from which to appreciate Stirling's unique position. To the north are the Ochil Hills, the closest being Dumyat. The southern aspect is dominated by Stirling and the castle. The Forth Valley and the river itself meander away to the east. To the west are the spectacular Trossachs and Loch Lomond.

The National Wallace Monument continues to be a thriving tourist attraction and a focus for national sentiment. In 1887 concerns were expressed in the local newspaper that it attracted too many visitors, and of the wrong sort, alcohol being much in evidence. Tourist numbers were not recorded until 1900, but in the early part of the twentieth century there were 20,000–25,000 annually, which rose steadily to 50,000 in 1994, 125,000 in 1996 and a reassuringly appropriate 200,000 or more in 2000. None of these figures include the many who climb the Abbey Craig for the free view (and why not) but do not enter the monument itself.

A typical tourist postcard of the late 1800s. The caption on the reverse says: 'The Wallace Monument is erected on a wooded hill just above Causewayhead, overlooking the waters of the Forth. It is only a short tram from Stirling, and is a popular excursion owing to the fine views of the surrounding country to be obtained from the top. A statue of the national hero has lately been added.' (*BD*)

Stirling Goes it Alone

In many ways, Stirling has had to plough its own furrow in developing arts and heritage attractions. Scotland suffers from a metropolitan frame of mind that tends to site everything important at either end of the Edinburgh Waverley–Glasgow Queen Steet rail line. This is perhaps not surprising when almost all political and cultural bodies are headquartered at one of these two poles and the vast majority of the Scottish population lives within their catchments.

Stirling has also suffered, as has the rest of Scotland, from a confused and often non-existent national tourism strategy which spent most of the final quarter of the twentieth century ignoring the evidence of what visitors wanted and constantly reinventing the structure, name and image of the lead tourism body. No one disagrees that Scotland is a modern, thriving country with unparalleled advantages in financial services, computing and call centres, but that isn't why visitors come. When they do come, they can find themselves swept up in the sanitised, pre-packaged 'culture' provided by the major hotel chains – heritage-on-a-stick and haggis-in-a-basket – served up to the sound of the bagpipes endlessly repeating 'Amazing Grace' (words by John Newton, English hymn writer and converted slave trader, tune courtesy of American plantation negroes) and Mull of Kintyre (by a Liverpudlian-Irish ex-Beatle). They are also peddled the convenient myths of Robert Bruce and 'find your clan tartan' ersatz genealogy. In tourism, as in war, truth is often the first casualty.

Stirling, perhaps because it comes under less influence of the Glasgow–Edinburgh axis, has resisted this trend more than most places and has taken the opportunity to present a coherent picture of itself as a growing community, rooted in the past but reaching for the future. Of course it is possible to buy cashmere, kilts and 'Celtic' jewellery, illuminated scrolls 'proving' your descent from some half-imagined clan chief and personalised whisky bottles. Nobody in their right commercial mind would resist the opportunity to turn a tourist coin or two. But amid the 'ghost walks' and 'living history' there is a genuine will to present Stirling in its proper context – not as a 'destination' (tourist board parlance for a place where the coach stops) but as a vibrant, happening, thoroughly modern city with a strong and interesting historical hinterland. Recently, Hollywood has provided an unexpected boost for tourism. The films *Braveheart*, *The Bruce* and *Rob Roy* have renewed interest in Stirling in much the same way that Scott and Stevenson's novels had in the nineteenth century.

For tourism purposes, Stirling is considered part of a larger area of Argyll, the Isles, Loch Lomond and the Trossachs. Now visitors make more than 1.5 million day trips to the area and almost 7 million overnight stays, spending nearly £250 million and which provides employment for 15,000 people in related jobs, about 10 per cent of the total workforce. Stirling Castle itself sees 400,000 people visit every year and is the fifth or sixth most popular paid tourist attraction in Scotland. Conscious of the need to keep the castle and its Great Hall in decent fettle, Historic Scotland has led a £20 million restoration and there are plans to restore the royal apartments of James V.

Other initiatives, including a £3 million extension to the Stirling Smith Art Gallery and Museum and the restoration and development of the seventeenth-century Guildhall, are in hand. The historic Tolbooth is now a modern arts resource centre with a theatre, dance studio, rehearsal space, recording studio, training facilities and a café-bar.

The focus in the new millennium is on environmentally sustainable tourism schemes, improved retail centres and the promotion of innovative performing and visual arts events, including an annual jazz festival, an experimental music festival, Le Weekend (international street theatre), castle concerts and The Gathering. Despite being virtually ignored by the Scottish Arts Council and other official bodies, Stirling continues to drive forward a progressive arts programme many larger towns and cities would be proud of.

In Stirling, there is more of the real Scotland – present as well as past – than in many other locations. There will no doubt be an additional upsurge in tourism as Scotland's new national parks come into play – the first based around Loch Lomond and the Trossachs and the next planned for the Cairngorms. This idea has taken more than a century to realise despite being invented by a Scot, John Muir, who was responsible for the national parks movement in the USA. Until now, Scotland was the only country in the world except Iraq to lack such a resource. While Stirling is outwith the official area of the Loch Lomond and Trossachs park, the council played an important part in shaping its conception and will doubtless reap some of the visitor benefits.

7

The Twentieth Century

The Christie Memorial Clock stands at the junction of Melville Terrace and Park Terrace at the entrance to the city, near the previous Barras Yett (burgh gate) and where the gallows once stood. It was presented by Ellen Christie in 1902 to Stirling Town Council in memory of her late husband George, a prominent local businessman, Provost of Stirling and Provincial Grand Master of the Masonic lodge, who died suddenly on a business trip to London. The clock bears an inscription commemorating his time as provost and the base has Masonic jewels and insignia. But its true significance is deeper – it is a parting memorial to the end of the Victorian era and the start of a new century. It is hard to imagine today the widow of an entrepreneur donating something as static as a piece of statuary – a charitable foundation would be more likely. Equally, what significance would Freemasonry have nowadays? Hardly any. It is doubtful whether anyone would get away with erecting the strangely androgynous statue called 'The Black Boy', or would even want to. And would an enlightened city administration accept such a thing if it were offered? Unlikely. Times have changed, and the hands of the Christie Clock sweep their passing.

Still at the Centre of Things

The early 1900s saw a number of trends emerging which flowered as the century progressed. Housing stock increased to cope with the expanding population, but, as with most of Scotland, the provision was originally patchy and not always of the highest quality. Manufacturing jobs have been largely supplanted by the service sector, as elsewhere, and it is a sign of the times that banks have become bars and supermarkets operate as banks, while petrol stations become corner shops and retailers cluster together in malls, just as they used to gather in market squares.

Stirling has retained its commercial and retailing activity and has also become increasingly reliant on tourism, local government and education. Home trades like weaving and small-scale production have given way to industries in purpose-built factories. But new businesses and commercial

Henry Campbell Bannerman MP, Prime Minister 1905–8. Just as the twentieth century started with a Stirling-based Prime Minister, the twenty-first saw the ex-leader of Stirling Council, Jack McConnell, become First Minister of the Scottish Parliament. (*Stirling Council*)

The Christie Memorial Clock and the Blade Boy Fountain. (*Stirling Council*)

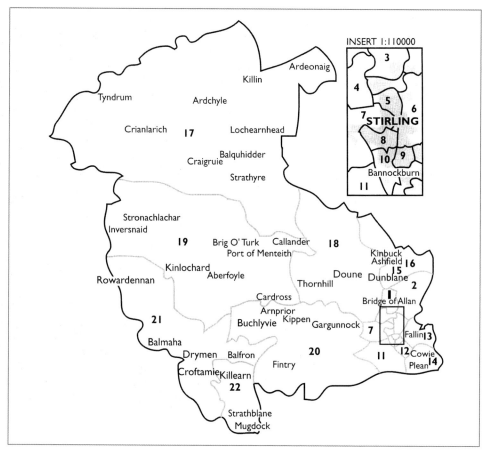

Stirling Council area is large and diversified. It covers 850 square miles – an area the size of Luxembourg – from Tyndrum in the southern Highlands to the north-west and Killin in the north-east, to Inversnaid in the west, Strathblane and Killearn in the south-west and the former mining villages of Fallin, Cowie and Plean in the south-east. The city itself is home to some 30,000 people, with 85,000 in the area as a whole: 60,000 urban (mainly in Stirling, Bridge of Allan and Dunblane) and 25,000 rural. The numbered wards in the map seen here refer to: 1. Bridge of Allan, 2. Logie, 3. Wallace, 4. Raploch, 5. Town Centre, 6. Argyll, 7. King's Park & Cambusbarron, 8. Torbrex, 9. Broomridge, 10. Borestone, 11. Bannockburn West, 12. Bannockburn East, 13. Polmaise, 14. Sauchenford, 15. Dunblane West, 16. Dunblane East, 17. Highland, 18. Teith, 19. Trossachs, 20. Campsies, 21. Strathendrick, 22. Blane Valley. (*Stirling Council*)

sectors have also emerged and today – in contrast to the shoe makers and bakers of the medieval period – the seven most important economic sectors in Stirling are, in no particular order: the public sector, education, tourism and transport, hotels and catering, retail, financial and information services, construction and manufacturing. Of these retail is the largest by a long way, although local shops and department stores have given way to chain multiples.

The trend towards large retail establishments was started by the Victorians and continued with chain stores like Woolworths arriving in 1924 and Marks & Spencer in the 1930s. But retail rationalisation in the 1970s and 1980s saw the true demise of many family businesses and the growth of mall shopping. In 1975, almost a century after the arcade opened, Stirling received its second

The Thistle Centre, Stirling's modern shopping mall, seen here soon after opening in 1975. It has since been joined by the Thistle Marches. (*SEFV*)

Driving sheep to market down Murray Place – this is no longer the common sight it once was. (*SCLS*)

purpose-built shopping complex – the Thistle Centre. A further £48 million development, the Thistle Marches, opened in 1997 and the number of people shopping there is a reported 400,000 a week. Like the shopping districts of many other Scottish towns, the malls contain mainly chain stores and franchises, as well as specialised shops aimed at the tourist market – woollen goods, tartans, artworks and contemporary Scottish jewellery. The more mundane shopping has been relegated to the superstores further out of town.

Industry

The industrial age, which saw Scotland become metal basher and boiler maker to the world, was with us for about 200 years and the burgh played its part in producing, fabricating and exporting. Ochil silver and copper, water to drive the mills, the local coal seams which powered the Industrial Revolution and the renowned weaving and dyeing industries were all significant. Stirling was never involved in heavy engineering to any degree, but played its part in metal goods manufacture – nails at St Ninians, pistol making at nearby Doune and a number of small foundries. However, by the twentieth century most of these small-scale industries had disappeared.

But new industries were not ignored. The Barnwells started the design and manufacture of aeroplanes at their Grampian Motor Works, although aeroplane manufacture never became a significant industry in Stirling. However, the local expertise in coachbuilding did not go to waste – Alexander's bus company diversified from selling bicycles and operating coaches to building bus bodies and – during the Second World War – military vehicles at their Forth Street and Drip Road sites. In 1953 Cape Insulation

Alexander's made bus bodies at Camelon and later Drip Road, Stirling, during the 1930s and after the Second World War before leaving for Camelon again in 1958. This picture is of the Midland Scottish depot at Bannockburn.

Where once there was agriculture and marsh, now there are business parks. Springkers and Castle Park, seen here, are examples of modern, spacious industrial and business units. (*SEFV*)

The site of Forthside, the new development aimed at transforming Stirling's centre. (*SEFV*)

A large proportion of the University of Stirling's £55 million annual turnover comes from research and the activities of the Innovation Park, home to almost forty technology based companies and housed in suitably modern buildings. (*SEFV*)

started the manufacture of mineral wool insulation at the Rocksil Works in Kerse Road and brought even more jobs to the area when it moved its head office from London in 1969. In the 1950s the cigarette factory opened. Initially owned by British American Tobacco, it was taken over by Imperial Tobacco. When the factory ceased to be economic, the company gifted it and the site to a trust which built the Stirling Enterprise Park. Gestetner opened a manufacturing facility in Causewayhead in the early 1970s, Wang Computers set up a factory close to the university in 1983 and Nexfor's MDF manufacturing plant is one of the largest in Britain.

Stirling has an industrial estate for light manufacturing, but most of the growth is in the new business parks built in the shadow of the castle. At the end of the twentieth century, one of Stirling's biggest employers was Scottish Amicable (now Prudential), based at Craigforth since 1957. This reflects the general shift away from manufacturing towards service industries.

The 'Information Society' is a couple of generations old and nearing full maturity. Many local companies either depend on or are involved in fostering the digital economy. Already more people travel into Stirling to work than travel out of it. As transport and communications improve and more and more people find they can work at home and travel only when necessary and convenient, an increasing number will choose to relocate to what is surely one of the most congenial parts of the country to live, work and play. Already there are industrial and business parks for electronics, software, telecommunications and financial services.

The next great development – the bio-informatics economy based on the explosive advances in genetic engineering and molecular biology – will make itself felt from about the year 2015. Stirling, already host to the University Innovation Park and sitting at a physical and informational crossroads, will

Stirling's greatest asset is still its geography. Neither Edinburgh nor Glasgow, a motorway network connects it readily with both while offering the advantages of more realistic property prices for businesses and their employees. It is as easy for a foreign traveller landing at Edinburgh or Glasgow airports to reach Stirling as, say, Dundee or Cumbernauld. (*SEFV*)

find itself at the hub of this activity, if it plays its cards right. This in turn will necessitate a greater number of service-based industries, improved retail facilities and expanded social infrastructure and public amenities – education, health, leisure and transport.

Leisure and Transport

There is no question that the vast majority of the populace is better off than ever before, and therefore has more time and money to devote to leisure. Play itself is an important economic activity. The leisure consumer society, a product of the downsizing in the aftermath of the greedy, workaholic 1980s, is marked by an almost manic desire to enjoy oneself – in theme pubs, clubs, tourist destinations and entertainment complexes – and Stirling has proved itself up to the challenge of meeting these needs. The creation of the Loch Lomond and Trossachs National Park to the west in 2002 will doubtless focus the tourism spotlight even more brightly on Stirling in the years to come.

The 'Town Hall' Theatre in Crawford's Arcade and the Olympia Picture Hall might be gone, but the Albert Halls remain and are host to many events. To add to this, Stirling Castle is now a noted site for concerts, with artists as diverse as Bob Dylan and Runrig appearing. In its first year as a new city Stirling has built on the international success of Le Weekend with a festival of music traditions in spring, plans for a children's festival in autumn and one with the theme of hogmanay. The macrobert, long established as an arts venue on the university campus, has also undergone a redevelopment. With the emphasis on children and families, it has performance space, a gallery and a film theatre.

Transport has also transformed the economy. The coming of the railways in Victorian times and later road building changed the focus of communications. Stirling, once a bustling port, now sits on one of the least-used stretches of

Opposite: Stirling has an almost bewildering variety of arts and leisure venues which is paying off in terms of attracting tourists and day visitors. There are often criticisms of the new uses found for old buildings but the Tolbooth has won several architectural awards for its design. This has revitalised not only the buildings, but also a part of town that was in danger of stagnating. (*Stirling Council*)

The artist of this appealing 1900s postcard is unknown, as is the identity of the lady exciting such interest or the reason for her visit to Stirling. (*BD*)

navigable river in the entire developed world. People want to drive. Stirling is at
the nexus of a road system that puts more than half of Scotland's population
within one hour's travel via the M9 and M876. The bus station sees over
200,000 departures each year and the trains put Glasgow and Perth within
half an hour's reach and Edinburgh less than an hour away. Stirling's greatest
asset is still its geography. Neither Edinburgh nor Glasgow, a motorway
network connects it readily with both while offering the advantages of more
realistic property prices for businesses and their employees.

New Build, New Homes

From a population of 12,000 in the 1870s, Stirling had almost 20,000 by
the early 1900s. The necessary urban growth to accommodate this expansion
took a different pattern from many other cities – Glasgow, for instance, threw
up slum tenements. Stirling made the best of what it had within the burgh
walls, then expanded outwards when it had to.

Originally, the Top of the Town had developed to house nobles, burgesses
and others who wanted, for reasons of convenience and influence, to be close
to the castle and Tolbooth. Later the Georgian town centre evolved beyond the
city walls to service the growing merchant class. However, the late Victorian
period saw many of the older buildings near the castle remodelled and what
spare ground there was put to use. The land surrounding Cowane's House
and the Spittal Hospital was sold for development. The Spittal and Allan
Hospital lands were given over mostly to low-density middle-class houses with
large gardens, in the area of King's Park. Doctors and lawyers congregated
there. The Cowane properties to the north made more of an impact on lower-
income families, with skilled artisans, teachers and other professionals
accommodated in the Wallace Street, George Street and Forth Crescent areas,
and the tenements around Cowane Street and Bruce Street. But the less-well-
heeled had to make do with the space vacated by these in the older properties
at the Top of the Town, just as had happened in Edinburgh's Old Town when
the better-off decanted to the New Town on the other side of Princes Street.

There were occasional dark mutterings at the time that those in control of
land and buildings did not necessarily have the interests of the lower orders
closest to their hearts. The owners of ex-hospital lands wanted the maximum
feus without the administrative problems of collecting rents, developers were
concerned to build high-value properties and many of the councillors were
the owners of land and property at the Top of the Town and therefore had a
vested interest in attracting as many rentals as possible. Nevertheless, there
was some lower-income building and occasional flashes of social conscience.
John Christie, a Stirling councillor, tried his best to instigate subsidised
working-class housing, but ultimately failed.

Added to this, the coal industry was attracting large numbers of miners
and their families from the west of Scotland and Ireland. Colliery rows erected
in Bannockburn and elsewhere were not always suitable (in 1893 Stirling
Council threatened to condemn one such development in Plean before the
houses were even occupied, requiring the owners to put in drains, ashpits and

Opposite: This aerial
photograph was taken
in the late 1980s and
shows a number of
changes that took place
at about that time. The
intriguingly shaped old
people's home on the
left sits beside Well
Green Business Park,
the gasometer on the
right is no longer there
and the site facing it is
now the Thistle Marches
shopping complex.
Beside it is the Forthside
area and the site of
what is now the Castle
Business Park can be
seen at the top of the
photograph. Compare
this with the image on
pp. 142–3. (*Stirling
Council*)

privies) and the Top of the Town became even more crowded and insanitary as a consequence. It took a combination of political pressure from the newly formed Labour Representation Committee and the legal requirements of the 1903 Burgh Police Act to make Stirling Council observe the laws about maximum occupancy. However, when buildings were found to be overcrowded, the miscreants were simply evicted, with nowhere else to go. This was less of a solution than an exacerbation of the situation. While the council saw fit to consider erecting itself a new municipal building at the corn exchange, the larger problem was ignored. It was pointed out that the projected £12,000 spend on civic convenience would build 100 homes. As if to rub the public's nose in it, King George V was invited to lay the foundation stone in 1914. Pressure to provide adequate housing was now at its height. But before this could be resolved, war was declared.

The part played by Stirling in the First World War is dealt with below but it is worth noting that it had a direct effect on housing conditions. Across the country the poor health of army recruits was blamed on inadequate social conditions and prompted the Housing Act of 1919. This allowed subsidised housing by the levy of a rate of $\frac{4}{5}$ of a penny in the pound with the remainder of the cost claimed from the government. Stirling, like many other councils, jumped at this (so much so that after handing over more than £20 million in three years, the government baulked and increased the supplement to be paid from local funds) and council housing started to appear. In the 20 years between the wars, Stirling managed to erect over 2,100 new houses, mainly at Bannockburn Road, Riverside, Lower Castlehill and particularly at Raploch. Other developments between the wars included more private housing – largely around the site of the present infirmary, itself opened in 1928 – and out towards Causewayhead, Bridge of Allan and St Ninians.

However, the demolition of the admittedly ruined buildings in St Mary's Wynd, Broad Street and the surrounding area caused an outcry among antiquarians and activists alike. One consequence of this was the establishment, in 1928, of the Thistle Trust, the first of its kind in Scotland, dedicated to acquiring, restoring, modernising and re-letting old buildings. The council was resolutely against this from the outset and finally, in 1952, made a compulsory purchase of the Trust's portfolio and demolished most of it. Therefore, 'Historic Old Stirling' as we see it today is largely a post-1945 re-creation. It's fair to say that today's Stirling Council would take a radically different approach and would attempt to preserve and improve rather than simply bulldoze.

Similarly, public-sector building after the Second World War was often erratic and ill-considered. Stirling made further great efforts at Raploch, Cornton, Linden Avenue and in other areas with prefabs, Atholl steel houses and other temporary structures and, as elsewhere in Scotland, the Scottish Special Housing Association provided new builds. But construction came to a virtual standstill during hostilities – Raploch had uncompleted houses throughout the 1939–45 period – so there was a need for post-war increase in the housing stock. It is generally recognised that the national building programme of the late 1940s and early 1950s was wholly inadequate.

New uses for old buildings. The Boy's Club was converted from the Butter Market in 1929 using architect Eric Bell's plans, which included crow-stepped gables and other traditional features. Now home to the Boys Brigade, Scouts and other youth organisations, it bears the uplifting mottos above the doors and windows: 'Keep Smiling. Play the Game. Stop Quarrelling'. (NP)

The legacy of the post-war housing boom was less than attractive 'schemes' which are now hard to let and impossible to sell. The famous flat-roofed Headridge bungalow, pioneered in Stirling, was not successful and from the 1960s there was an increasing demand for private homes. But urban regeneration projects are under way for a great deal of Stirling's public housing stock, including redevelopment of Raploch with 800 new homes and other improved facilities.

Today, Stirling's shape and nature is changing to reflect different needs. Disused railway sidings, army barracks and redundant Ministry of Defence land is being reshaped as Forthside, which at over 40 acres and a cost of some £90 million is one of the largest public/private sector developments in Scotland. It will mix retailing with exhibition space, a muliplex cinema, a hotel and a network of riverside footpaths, as well as a new civic square in front of the railway station.

Wars and After

Stirling fared better than many parts of Britain during the two world wars. The strategic siting which was its very *raison d'être* in earlier centuries was all but irrelevant during one war fought largely in France and the next conducted from the air. The Forth Bridge was a more important target for bombers, and Stirling had none of the heavy industry such as shipbuilding or munitions which led to the large-scale bombings of Glasgow, Greenock, Rosyth and elsewhere. In many ways, Stirling's lack of dependence on large manufacturing was its saving grace between and after the wars, whereas other areas took the brunt of unemployment, depression and slump.

THOSE MAGNIFICENT BARNWELLS IN THEIR FLYING MACHINES

Frank and Harold Barnwell were aviation pioneers who gave their lives to aircraft design, and lost them in the same cause, as did Frank's three sons. The success of the Wright Brothers in the USA inspired a number of Scots engineers to venture into aviation by creating their own designs or by copying those of Bleriot or Farman, but the Barnwell brothers were the most successful. Frank and Harold designed and constructed their first monoplane at their Causewayhead engineering works in 1908.

Powered by a 40hp twin-cylinder air-cooled engine it only achieved a take-off run of 25mph rather than the 35mph needed, and failed to fly. Their second attempt, a biplane, had limited success. It was a canard design (tail-first) with a 48-foot wingspan, powered by a four-cylinder Humber car engine driving two propellers 10 feet in diameter. A few short flights were achieved but the design was abandoned in favour of their third model, which in 1911 won the Scottish Aeronautical Society Law Prize worth £50 for the first Scottish half-mile flight and later exceeded 5 miles flying at Blair Drummond. Frank Barnwell also designed the 40hp twin-cylinder water-cooled engine which powered it.

Barnwell wrote a well-known book, *Aeroplane Design*, in 1909, which took the reader step-by-step through the design of an airplane, and an appendix by W.H. Sayers summarised everything known about aircraft stability at that time.

Harold Barnwell, the less-famous brother but the better aviator, in a rather grainy photograph from 1910 or 1911. (*BD*)

Frank and Harold then moved south. Frank joined Sir George White's British and Colonial Aeroplane Company (later the Bristol Aeroplane Company) where he designed some of the most famous and widely used aircraft of both world wars and his pioneering ideas led directly to Sir Archibald Russell's groundwork for Concorde. Harold went to Vickers, where he was killed in a flying accident in 1917. Frank was at Bristol for the rest of his career, apart from a short-lived stint as a captain in the army until 1915. But he was worth more at home. He was Bristol's experimental designer 1911–14, Chief Designer 1915–21 and 1923–36 and chief engineer from 1936 until his death in 1938.

Frank Barnwell designed many famous planes for Bristol, including the Scout biplane, the Fighter (more popularly called the 'Brisfit' or 'Biff', one of the outstanding planes of the First World War), and the Bristol F2 (which remained in production long after the end of the war and was still in service with the RAF in 1932). Barnwell's early designs also set the scene for the production of many other famous aircraft, like the Bulldog and the Blenheim, mainstay of the RAF's operations in the first three years of the Second World War. In 2001 the last flyable Bristol Blenheim made a commemorative run over its designer's old home ground at Stirling.

Frank Barnwell was an enthusiastic pilot, but not a good one. He was banned from flying any of the Bristol Company's aeroplanes for his own safety, but he built his own personal plane and was killed in August 1938 while testing it at Bristol Civil Airport, Whitchurch. Frank's three sons all died flying in the Second World War.

Stirling has a long history of flight, from Damian's attempt at the castle in 1507 and Charles Green's balloon flight in 1831 to the Barnwells and beyond. The monoplane designed by Harold and Frank Barnwell had its first test run at Cornton Farm, Stirling, on 4 December 1908. They won a prize with a later design in 1911, the same year as the *Daily Mail* Round Britain Race from London to King's Park, Stirling, and back, which is seen here. The Barnwells did not compete, but helped out, as did the local Scout troop. (*BD*)

Practically the only direct casualty of the hostilities was King's Park, the senior football team in Stirling prior to the Second World War. Under Secretary-Manager Tom Fergusson (whose playing career ended when he lost a leg in the First World War) the club had been debt-ridden and mired in controversy for years. The German bomb that fell on Forthbank was the final straw. However, keen to have senior football in the burgh, Fergusson and other local businessmen decided to form a new club after the war and chose to call it Stirling Albion, reputedly after the lorries Fergusson used in his coal-merchant business. Known for years as 'Mr Stirling Albion', Fergusson served as a director, secretary, chairman and even manager at various times through the 1950s and 1960s, and ran the team from his premises in Wallace Street.

However, Stirling did play a vital part in both wars – as the home of the Argyll and Sutherland Highlanders and a major contributor of soldiers to its ranks. In addition, during the Second World War, Stirling's public buildings were requisitioned for the usual admixture of wartime roles – Airthrey Castle was an evacuee centre, Allan's School a supply depot for medical stores and St Mary's School a prisoner-of-war camp (as, briefly, was Westerton House in Bridge of Allan).

The town also had a significant connection with the RAF – 43 Squadron was founded in Stirling in 1916 based around 19 Reserve Squadron and their biplanes flew from Fallenich Farm, in the castle's shadow. Over 150 Royal Flying Corps personnel were stationed in Stirling. It took almost a year for 43 Squadron to reach the Western Front where it was re-equipped with Sopwith Camels.

After the war, the squadron moved to Germany, briefly, returning to Stirling in August 1919 when it was disbanded. However, Stirling became the headquarters of the RAF in Scotland, based at the Station Hotel. But it was eventually considered to have no future as an airbase. According to Sir Alan Cobham: 'the disadvantages of Stirling are concerned with the high land that surrounds it – in other words the Castle Rock is in the way'.

Re-formed at Northolt in 1925 under Squadron Commander A.F. Brook, 43 Squadron flew Spitfires in the Second World War and has been based at Leuchars in Fife since 1945. In May 2002, four Tornado jet fighters from 43 Squadron performed a fly-past over the castle, following Queen Elizabeth's visit to Stirling when it became Scotland's newest city.

The University of Stirling

In 1967 the new University of Stirling was founded near Bridge of Allan on the other side of the River Forth and continues to grow while remaining possibly Europe's most beautifully sited campus.

As early as 1617 King James VI had suggested that there be a 'free university' in Stirling. It took exactly 350 years to realise his idea. The 1963 Robbins Report recommended there be a new university in Scotland, and it was agreed that it should be built in Stirling, precisely because of its location – midway between east and west, north and south. The location chosen was

FROM CROWN LAND TO UNIVERSITY

Airthrey is first recorded in a charter of David I and other twelfth-century documents as Atherai or Atheran. The name is possibly a corruption of Ard-rhedadie – 'high or sheer road', a reference to the old and very steep path leading to Sheriffmuir – or from Airthrin – 'sharp point' or 'conflict'. This might refer to the battle fought near the site in 839 when the Picts were defeated by Kenneth MacAlpin's Scots.

The estate was Crown land until 1370 when it was granted to Sir John Herice, Keeper of Stirling Castle. In 1645, during the fighting between the Royalists and the Covenanters, the manor house of Airthrey was burned to the ground and the estate remained in various hands until 1706 when it was sold to Ralph Dundas, whose son John built Airthrey House in 1748. The next owner was Captain Robert Haldane of Plean whose son Robert commissioned a design for a castle from Robert Adam in 1791, built a 4-mile-long stone wall around the perimeter and developed the gardens. A bit of a joker, Haldane erected a hermitage and advertised for a real hermit. One applied, but didn't meet the conditions – he wouldn't promise to stay out of contact with the outside world.

Haldane was also easily bored. In 1798, not long after the castle's completion, he sold the estate for £46,000 to Sir Robert Abercrombie, who moved the village of Logie to its new site in Causewayhead and 'discontinued' the village of Pathfoot. This was a community of shoe makers and cordwainers and all that remained of the village was the standing stone where its annual fair was held. In 1889 Aithrey was bought by the Graham family who later gave it over to the Secretary of State for Scotland as a maternity hospital. Stone from the Airthrey House stable, demolished for the siting of the house, was used in the restoration of Stirling Castle from 1964.

Airthrey Castle, built in 1791 to designs by Robert Adam, is now the home of the University of Stirling. (*SCLS*)

The University of Stirling, widely held to be Europe's most visually stunning campus, was founded on the Airthrey estate and opened for business in 1967. In the years following, the campus extended around the loch. The macrobert arts centre, the hub of Stirling's cultural life, opened in 1970 with facilities for film, dance, theatre, music and exhibitions. Sports are strong at the University of Stirling. The Gannochy Centre has a gym, swimming pool, badminton and squash courts, athletics track and playing fields. It is a recognised tennis centre of excellence and the headquarters of the Scottish Institute of Sport and the Scottish National Swimming Academy. These facilities are also available to the public. (*University of Stirling*)

Doubtless the landmark building is the principal's house, possibly the finest modern house in Scotland. It was built to the specifications of the first principal Dr Tom Cottrell. His brief to the architects was to maximise daylight and wall space, the better to display works of art. Perched on a wooded hillside with a courtyard, the L-shaped construction provides stunning views across the campus. Dr Cottrell, every bit as progressive in the visual arts and design as in education, also persuaded the government that 1 per cent of the university's building costs should go towards the purchase of modern art and sculpture for the campus. His 'Per Cent for Art' concept has subsequently been adopted by many other bodies, including Stirling Council. (*University of Stirling*)

the grounds of the former Airthrey estate and its 360 acres of park and woodland with a loch. The University of Stirling opened in 1967 and now has 8,500 students from 75 countries.

The name of the first project on the site, the Pathfoot Building, commemorated the long-vanished village which was 'discontinued' by Sir Robert Abercrombie when he bought the estate in 1798. In the years following, the campus extended around the loch. The MacRobert Arts Centre, now renamed macrobert, the hub of Stirling's cultural life, opened in 1970 with facilities for film, dance, theatre, music and exhibitions. Sports are also strong at the university and the Gannochy Centre has a gym, swimming pool, badminton and squash courts, athletics track and playing fields. It is a recognised tennis centre of excellence and the headquarters of the Scottish Institute of Sport and the Scottish National Swimming Academy. These facilities are also open to the public. The Innovation Park is hailed as a model of university–industry cooperation.

Scotland's Newest City

Stirling continues to be a town of contrasts – high employment but low wages; low productivity but high business growth; less deprivation than elsewhere but a greater than average disparity between richest and poorest; a growing population but much of it commuters and retired people; Scotland's newest city and home to its oldest inhabitant (Lucy D'Abreu, born in India in 1892). Measures are in hand to attract more companies in the electronics and financial services sectors as these are seen to be the key industries that will increase average wages, currently dominated by retail, catering and the public sector. Already over forty high-tech companies are based at the University of Stirling's Innovation Park and the Castle Business Park is home to the Bank of Bermuda, Highland Distillers and Prudential among others. And, of course, Stirling is still the major staging post for tourists exploring the Highlands.

However, through all the changes of the last few millennia since someone first thought the castle rock was a good, safe place to build a fire, Stirling has managed to retain its historic character, which was doubtless in its favour when it became Scotland's sixth city in 2002 in honour of HM Queen Elizabeth's Golden Jubilee. It is unclear what benefits city status will confer on Stirling – other than publicity and local pride, neither of which is a bad thing. Officially Scotland's safest city, Stirling is a major 'Quality of Life' award winner and its schools figure in the top three of attainment league tables. With £140 million public and private investment in the last decade of the twentieth century, it now has Scotland's highest number of business start-ups, an above-average business survival rate and, according to a Fraser of Allander report, the country's highest number of entrepreneurs. With all this, as well as the plethora of arts events, community programmes, regeneration projects and almost £2 million from a cities scheme in 2003, Stirling looks sure to face the future with confidence. The 'bliss of grenial air and fertile fields' has given way to a renewed sense of place and worth and a forward-looking attitude. The kings and queens are gone and the battles long-since fought. But the castle rock endures, as do the people who draw their strength from it. Stirling? there's no place like it.

Previous pages: This aerial photograph of the city was taken in 2002. Compare it with the image on p. 135. Most prominent here are the Thistle Centre, Thistle Marches and the Forth Side development. (*Stirling Council*)

ELIZABETH THE SECOND, by the Grace of God of the United Kingdom of Great Britain and ✧ ✧ Northern Ireland and of Our other Realms and Territories, QUEEN, Head of the Commonwealth Defender of the Faith, to all whom these Presents shall come, GREETING! Whereas We for ✧ ✧ divers good causes and considerations Us thereunto moving are graciously pleased to confer on the Town of Stirling the Status of a City. Now Therefore Know Ye that We of Our especial grace and ✧ ✧ favour and mere motion do by these Presents ordain, declare and direct that the Town of Stirling shall ✧ ✧ henceforth have the status of a City and shall have all such rank, liberties, privileges and immunities as are incident to a City; IN WITNESS WHEREOF We have ordered the Seal appointed by the Treaty of Union to be kept and made use of in place of the Great Seal of Scotland to be appended hereto. GIVEN at Our Court at St. James's the Twenty Second day of April in the year Two Thousand and Two and in the Fifty First year of Our Reign.

PER·SIGNATURAM·MANU·S.D.N.·REGINAE·SUPRA·SCRIPTAM.

Stirling was granted city status in 2002, one of five British towns to receive the honour, as part of the celebrations for HM the Queen's Golden Jubilee. The Queen visited Stirling on Friday 24 May and presented the Letters Patent, seen here, which created Scotland's newest city. The other cities were Preston in England, Newport in Wales and Lisburn and Newry in Northern Ireland. Exeter became a Lord Mayoralty. (*Stirling Council*)

Acknowledgements & Picture Credits

Many thanks are due to: Barbara Chalmers and John McPake of Stirling Council, without whom all of this would have taken a lot longer; to Elspeth King of the Stirling Smith Art Gallery and Museum; to Stirling Council Library Services; to the University of Stirling's Judith Gray and Alan Forrester; to Pam Reitsch; to Jackie Reid and Claire Carter of Scottish Enterprise Forth Valley; to Michael L. Jex; and to Sarah and Reuben, who went out on a limb for this book. A special mention is due to Andrew Jennings, bookseller of Bridge of Allan, a scholar and a gentleman.

As ever, Natasha walked it with me and took photographs, while Anna and Jamie gave me the space to do it. And to all those who gave me access to their time, their knowledge, their collections and libraries and wanted no other acknowledgement – you know who you are and you have my gratitude.

All translations from the Latin are by the author, and all consequent mistakes his alone.

Pictures used are acknowledged in the captions as follows: Stirling Council, Stirling Council Library Services (SCLS); University of Stirling, Scottish Enterprise Forth Valley (SEFV). The images used in this book are the copyright and property of these bodies, where so marked, and are used here with the copyright owners' permissions. Pictures marked BD are from the personal collections of the author and those marked NP are the property and copyright of Dr Nataliya Pisareva. Other images are believed to be in the public domain and if not, have been used inadvertently.

INDEX

Italics refer to colour plates.